Cursive Stroke

Penmanship

for Christian Writing

Penmanship

for Christian Writing

Grade 2

Teacher's Manual

Rod and Staff Publishers, Inc.
P.O. Box 3, Hwy. 172
Crockett, Kentucky 41413
Telephone: (606) 522-4348

Acknowledgements

We acknowledge that our omniscient, ever-present Lord has provided us the opportunity and understanding for a venture of this sort. Working closely together, those involved have been enabled by God to establish this new Penmanship series. Our desire has been to please the Lord in providing this course for the Christian school.

We also acknowledge that we have benefited from other handwriting systems in developing the system used in this series. And many teachers were also consulted.

Research and Writing—Daniel Strubhar

Final Editing—Marvin Eicher

Grade Two Curriculum

Pupil's Workbook Units 1, 2

Teacher's Manual

Rod and Staff Publishers, Inc.
Crockett, Kentucky 41413

Printed in U.S.A.

ISBN 0-7399-0563-5

Catalog no. 15291

13 14 15 16 17 — 17 16 15 14 13 12 11 10 09 08

Table of Contents

Unit 2 Cursive Writing

Introduction to Penmanship Series

Penmanship is a subject that many teachers have often overlooked. The reasons are many and varied; but no doubt the main reason is simply that other subjects are considered to be more important, and penmanship has been crowded into the background. But we feel that handwriting needs to hold a prominent place in our Christian school curriculums and that it needs to be taught in an orderly, thorough, and efficient manner. This is the basic reason behind the production of this handwriting series.

The Importance of Teaching Penmanship in Our Schools

1. Good penmanship is a mark of Christian carefulness. God expects His people to be thorough and exact in their activities, not slipshod and careless.

2. Good penmanship is a mark of Christian courtesy. Writing that is difficult to read will not be appreciated by those who must read it.

3. Good penmanship is necessary for good communication. Even though word processors and copiers have taken over in many areas of communication, there are still many purposes for writing that are better accomplished by means of handwriting.

4. Good penmanship is an aid to efficiency. Well-written messages are far less time-consuming to read than those poorly written.

5. Good penmanship will affect students' attitudes. If neat writing is insisted upon, the very act of penning words and sentences in a neat manner will cause students to want to do their best work.

6. Good penmanship on the part of our students will leave a good testimony for our school program. Penmanship is the first thing that impresses the critical eye, before the quality of the work done is apparent.

7. We need to teach good penmanship because it is right. We must do well whatever needs to be done. "Whatsoever thy hand findeth to do, do it with thy might" (Ecclesiastes 9:10).

Our Approach to Handwriting

1. Teaching by Strokes

Teaching handwriting by strokes is the simplest and most efficient way to get the principles of handwriting across. With this approach, the child learns and practices a few basic strokes from which most letters are composed. As he learns these strokes, he has a tool for conquering difficulties in letter formation. In practicing the strokes, he will also become better acquainted with the feel of the basic movements of handwriting, which will help his handwriting to become more efficient and more automatic.

The stroke approach is also beneficial from the teacher's standpoint. It gives him something to teach in handwriting, rather than allowing handwriting instruction to degenerate into nothing more than remedial work. It tends to give a greater enthusiasm for handwriting, because the teacher will know better how to teach it.

Here is how two typical letters are learned by the stroke method:

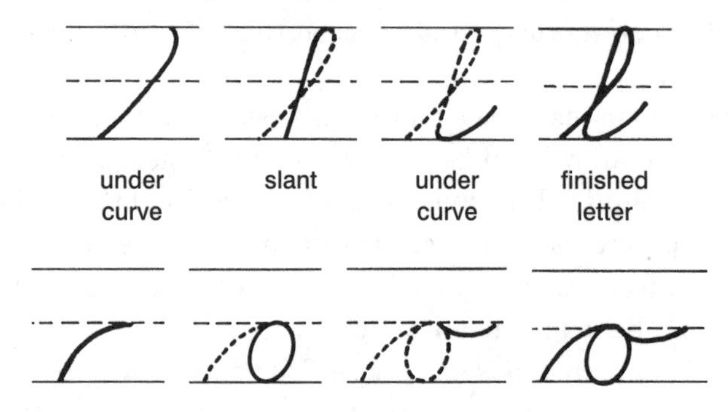

2. Teaching Quality

In this course we want to give considerable attention to the teaching of quality. Quality includes slant, alignment, size, proportion, line quality, and spacing, and is a very important part of handwriting (see diagrams and definitions below). The proper teaching of quality may spell the difference between success and failure in teaching handwriting. The teaching of quality should not be too far removed from the teaching of letter form, so that the children do not separate the two in everyday writing.

Definitions:

Slant—degree to which a letter is slanted

consistent slant—all letters slanted the same

correct slant—straight up and down for first grade manuscript; leaning forward for slant print and cursive

Alignment—tops and bottoms of letters in straight lines

Size—largeness or smallness of letters in comparison with what they should be (guidelines for size are specific in each grade)

Proportion—size of letters or letter parts in relation to other letters or letter parts

Line quality—degree of lightness or heaviness of writing, related to pencil pressure

Spacing—distance between words, letters, or sentences

Diagrams of the six areas of quality:

3. Difference in Emphasis at Various Grade Levels

In this course, we follow an emphasis at each grade level which builds upon the previous grade, while also reviewing a large part of the previous year's material. The first three grades contain the bulk of new material. For this reason, these grades are the most basic, and the teachers of these grades must be especially careful to give the children a right foundation in handwriting. Grade four contains the least new material. Quality should receive a greater emphasis in grades four to six, and the teachers of these three grades must put forth a continuous effort to keep the students' handwriting up to the standard. In seventh and eighth grades, teachers must emphasize speed, efficiency, and practical handwriting applications in everyday life, while still continuing an emphasis on handwriting quality.

Posture, Pencil Holding, and Paper Placement

Following are standards for proper posture, pencil holding, and paper placement:

1. Posture at seat
    a. Sit back in the seat.
    b. Sit up straight.
    c. Have feet flat on the floor.
    d. Lean slightly forward from the hips.
    e. Have one arm on desk, holding paper, while the other arm writes.

POSTURE

Sit and stand with your back straight and with both feet flat on the floor. Lean forward only a little when you sit at your desk.

2. Posture at blackboard
    a. Stand squarely on both feet directly in front of the blackboard.
    b. Stand back six to twelve inches from the blackboard.

3. Pencil holding
   a. Pencil should be held between the thumb and first finger, resting lightly on the second finger.
   b. Pencil should be held no more firmly than necessary for control.
   c. Pencil must not be cramped or pinched.
4. Chalk holding
   a. Chalk should be held firmly between thumb and first two fingers.
   b. Chalk should point toward the palm of the hand.

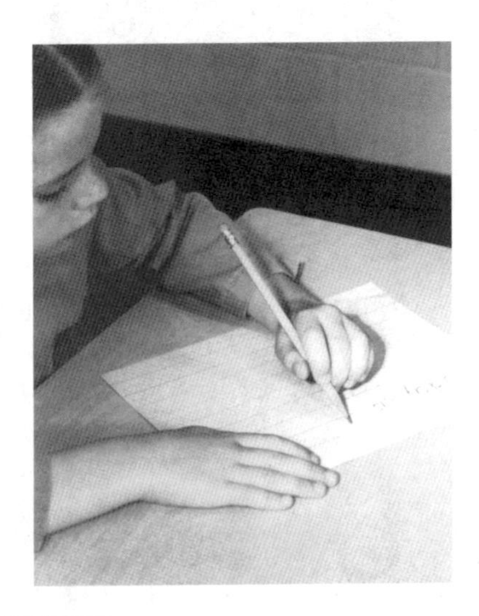

PENCIL HOLDING

Hold the pencil so that its top points back over your shoulder. Hold it tightly enough to control it, but do not pinch it.

5. Paper placement
   a. For vertical manuscript, paper should always be placed straight up and down on the desk top, except that left-handers should slant it to the right. For slant print and cursive writing, right-handers should slant the paper about thirty degrees to the left, and left-handers should slant it toward the right as taught in "Special Instructions for Left-handed Pupils."

b. The paper should be on the side of the desk toward the arm that will be used to write.

PAPER PLACEMENT

If you write with your right hand, slant the paper to the left. If you write with your left hand, slant the paper to the right far enough so that you can see your writing.

Special Instructions for Left-handed Pupils

Many teachers seem confused when it comes to teaching left-handed pupils how to write. How should they slant their papers and hold their pencils? How can they write so as to be able to see their writing? How does one prevent them from developing a hooked wrist? This section is intended to answer these questions with sound, positive directions for teachers of left-handers. Although some points may seem strange and even impractical, note carefully that *these principles were developed over several decades* of experimentation with left-handers in many schools. Those left-handers who learned to write by this method developed a neater, more even, and more efficient handwriting style than those taught by other methods. Therefore, unless your left-handed students have already formed poor writing habits, these principles will practically guarantee success if you diligently follow them.

A left-handed pupil must deal with a peculiar handicap when he learns to write. Writing moves from left to right; and for the left-handed person this means that his writing hand will cover his writing as he moves along. Therefore, many left-handers resort to what seems the simplest solution: a hooked wrist.

However, the hooked wrist is by no means the best solution to this problem. This method makes writing laboriously slow, inefficient, and unpleasant. A far better method is to teach left-handed pupils *from the start* that there are certain things they must do differently than right-handed pupils if they are to write well. These differences are listed here.

1. Instead of placing their papers vertically (or slanted to the left for cursive) on their desks, *left-handers must always slant their papers to the right.* In first grade their arms should meet the lines of their papers at right angles; later, *for cursive writing,* their arms should meet their papers *across the lower right-hand corner.* Although this much slant may seem extreme, experience has shown that this is the best way for left-handers to get the proper slant on their letters without using a hooked wrist.
2. *Left-handers should always write toward, not away from, themselves.* If they slant their papers properly, as outlined in number 1 above, they will naturally do this. But when they write

at the blackboard, you will need to make special provisions so that this is possible. *Therefore, give a left-handed child about twice as much room at the blackboard* as what you give to a right-handed child. Then, instead of writing in the space directly in front of him, he can start in the space to his left and write *toward himself* as a left-handed writer should.

3. *Left-handers should hold their pencils exactly the same way that right-handers do.* If they cannot see their writing, either they are holding the pencil too close to the point or their desks are too high. Left-handers can normally write better at a desk lower than usual, because they can better see over their writing hand that way.
4. *If you have a large number of left-handers, group them together* for penmanship classes if possible. This would be especially good in the lower grades, where handwriting habits are first being established. In this way they will not become confused as easily by the right-handers, and you can more quickly see whether they are developing proper habits. Place this group to the right side of the class (as you face the front) so that they can read, as well as write, *toward themselves.*
5. In slant printing and cursive writing, the left-hander's strokes are opposite of the right-hander's. The right-hander *pulls* downstrokes vertically *toward himself,* whereas the left-hander should *push* downstrokes horizontally *away from himself.* Also, the right-hander *pushes* across strokes horizontally *away from himself,* but the left-hander should *pull* across strokes vertically *toward himself.* Study this diagram carefully:

Left-hander

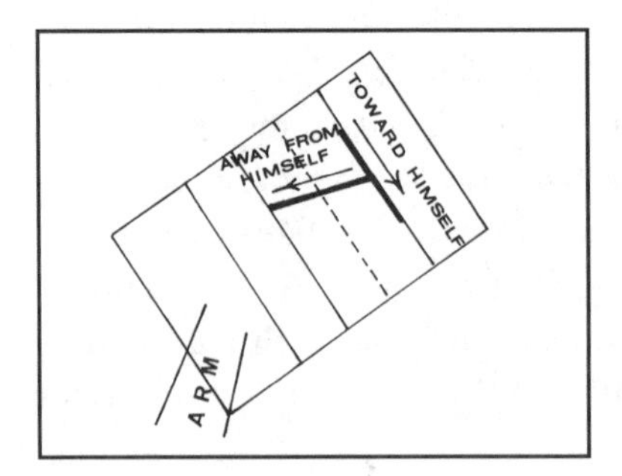

Right-hander

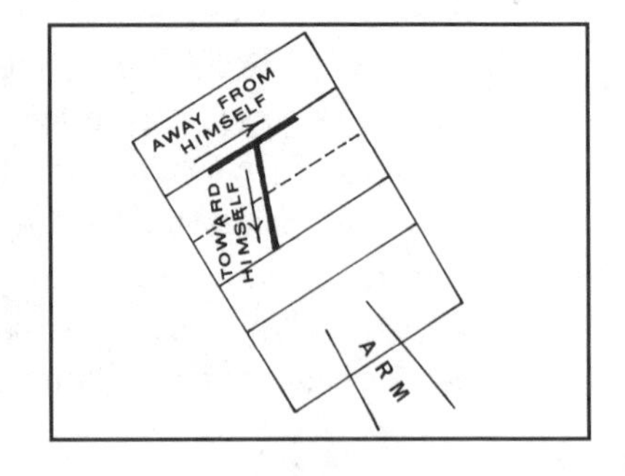

Again, do not be surprised if you have never heard of some of these points. Perhaps *your* teachers never heard of them either! Begin *now* to put them to use—and do so by all means if you are a first or second grade teacher. Then you will have the satisfaction of teaching by a definite method that works, and you will have begun on the road to successful handwriting for your left-handed pupils.

Illustrations for proper pencil holding, paper placement, and writing method for left-handed pupils are included in the section "Posture, Pencil Holding, and Paper Placement."

How to Treat the Teacher's Manual

In this course there are detailed instructions for each lesson. The teacher's manual gives direction to the teacher on what goals to strive for, how to fill out the workbooks, and how to conduct the class so that the children gain the clearest possible understanding of the lesson. It also gives other diagnostic, remedial, and informative suggestions. And each lesson in the teacher's manual has a reduction of the student workbook lesson, for your handy reference.

We suggest that you as a teacher do not overlook the teacher's manual in your preparation for class but that you study it carefully sometime previous to the class period. Especially the inexperienced teacher should read over it carefully and thoroughly. Do not let your teaching flounder because of a lack of understanding of the subject material and correct class procedure. Even an experienced teacher does well to study the teacher's manual, although he may already be able to teach the writing of the alphabet successfully. It will help him to understand the approach we are taking in the teaching of this course, and the sequence of thought throughout the lessons.

We suggest not only that you read the manual for each lesson a few hours previous to teaching it but also that you read ahead in the teacher's manual from time to time, to keep abreast of just where you are in accomplishing your goals for the year. You may also find that some of the suggestions that are given in future lessons may be helpful to you in the lessons you are presently teaching, even though they may not always be directly applicable to the present lesson.

Do not take for granted that just because something is not mentioned in the teacher's manual for a particular lesson, it is therefore not to be considered in that lesson. For example, not every lesson mentions that you should be sure your children practice correct posture and pencil-holding habits, but you should watch for this each day. Various items of this nature will be brought to your attention from time to time as reminders to keep watching these areas.

Finally, do not be a slave to your teacher's manual. You do not have to accept every suggestion or follow the exact procedure for every class period that is outlined, right down to saying the exact words that are suggested. The teacher's manual is there to guide the teacher's thinking and is not the final rule of procedure for every situation. However, the basic suggestions were included because they were felt to be important, and the teacher should consider and use them in one form or another as he plans the lesson.

To the Second Grade Teacher

In second grade you are continuing to build the learning structure upon the foundation established in first grade. You do not want any important building blocks missing in helping the children to build good, legible, and neat handwriting. Following are some of the "blocks" you will want to utilize in laying the "second row":

1. *Maintenance of correct habits of posture, pencil holding, and paper placement.* Reestablish these habits promptly at the beginning, and maintain them throughout the year.

2. *A good teacher example.* You should have good handwriting yourself. It will be difficult for you to teach penmanship with any degree of success unless you are able to apply handwriting principles to your own writing. Be willing to improve your handwriting if necessary.

3. *A good emphasis on review.* You should be aware of how well your children are retaining what they have been learning, and then emphasize continual review. Even when the lesson does not have a line of review, it would be good to take a few minutes to have them practice a formerly learned letter or stroke.

4. *Teaching each lesson well.* Never be satisfied until you are certain that the children are doing the best they can.

5. *Not allowing significantly poorer work in daily assignments than in the writing lesson.* The children should understand that what they learn in penmanship class must be applied in other subjects.

Course Organization and Goals

This course has sixty lessons and is organized into two units, each unit containing thirty lessons. The first unit deals with regular manuscript and slant print writing; the second unit deals with cursive writing.

The main goal of this second grade course is to help the children progress from regular manuscript writing to a fair understanding of the strokes and letters of cursive writing.

Time Spent in Writing Class

The curse is designed for two lessons per week for thirty weeks. This is not a full school year, but it is to aid you in having plenty of time to teach each lesson well. The lessons should be evenly spaced in the week, with approximately the same amount of time between each lesson. The children should be given one of the practice sentences (which are based on *Bible Nurture and Reader Series* reading) to write each morning as a warmup exercise on the days that you do not have penmanship class. Also, the children can be permitted to finish some lessons outside of class period if necessary.

Allow from fifteen to twenty minutes for each class. Yes, it does take time, but second grade is a basic learning grade. You must take the time to be sure the children learn the material well.

Conducting the Class Period

You should follow this basic procedure in teaching the strokes or letters of each lesson:

1. *Explain and demonstrate the letter on the blackboard.*

2. *Have the children practice the letter themselves on the blackboard* or on other paper as soon as possible after your demonstration.

3. *Have the children work the lesson* under your supervision. A star (*) before a paragraph indicates lesson directions for the pupil's page. Be sure you correct mistakes when you notice them either on an individual or class level.

4. *If you are not satisfied with the children's work, keep them practicing* until their work does come up to that which you consider satisfactory.

What Kind of Work Should You Expect?

You should expect the beginning second grader to do very accurate and neat work with regular manuscript writing, especially after a bit of refresher practice at the beginning of the year. After the middle of the year, he should also be able to write slant print accurately; and by the end of the year, he should be quite accurate with cursive small letters. By the term *accurate,* we mean with no major deviation from standard form. Any significant deviation from standard form should always be corrected immediately. Accept a few wavers, etc., in lines, although you should do all you can to help the children write smoothly. You do not need to expect that the children will remember how to form every cursive capital perfectly this year, though you should correct their errors even with cursive capitals.

Greater perfection with cursive capitals will come in third grade. However, the children should know that you are expecting them to do their very best in every area.

By the end of the year, the children should be able to form each cursive small letter neatly to the basic strokes.

Left-handed Pupils

Second grade children should already have their hand dominance fairly well established. So it is up to you to notice what the hand dominance of each child is and to respect it. Especially, you should not neglect the left-handed child, but be sure that he has correct habits. See "Special Instructions for Left-handed Pupils."

Evaluation and Grading

Evaluation involves looking over your child's paper for errors in form, neatness, and quality. In doing this, you should make notations on each child's paper, showing him what is wrong with his work and how he can improve.

Since second grade is learning mostly new work, you will want to be careful when you grade your children's papers. It is not fair to grade children on first-time work in penmanship. Rather, grade them on work that they have already learned at some previous time.

Grade the children on how well they are picking up the material and also on their mastery of form, quality, and neatness. Part of the grade should be based on your general evaluation of their progress, while part of the grade should be based on your specific evaluation of different aspects of writing. In those lessons that you grade, count each area of writing a certain part of the grade. Most important at this stage is proper formation of the letters. Count that as 50 points out of a total grade of 100 percent. Count neatness as 25 points of the grade, and quality (alignment and slant) as 25 points. As you check their work, subtract points for each area in which there are errors on inaccuracies.

Establish good standards for grading. Do not fall into the habit of giving an *A+* for an excellent paper, an *A* for an average paper, and an *A-* for a poor paper. That is almost meaningless. You should make your grades say something instead. If your children's grades are all in the very high or very low bracket, something may be wrong with your grading system.

Miscellaneous Helps

1. As an aid to your children when they practice on the blackboard, you should draw lines for them to write on. The simplest way is to use a staff liner. For second-grade writing size, it works well to remove the second and fourth pieces of chalk.

Another possibility is to use a felt-tip marker to make the lines. But since these lines will likely last for a fairly long time, you should probably consult your school board before doing this.

2. Remember the extra practice paper on the back side of each page, and do not hesitate to use it if you feel that your children need extra practice on paper. If more paper is needed, try to get paper that has lines which are similar to the lines in this book. (Available at Rod and Staff Publishers.)

3. Help the children to make the adjustment from writing paper with middle lines to writing paper that has only a bottom line as in other subjects besides penmanship. Explain to them that they need to learn to estimate the right height when there are no lines to guide them. They should try to make the letters proportioned the same as when there are middle lines.

Vertical Manuscript
Demonstration Strokes

a b c d e f g h i j k l m n

o p q r s t u v w x y z

A B C D E F G H I J

K L M N O P Q R S T

U V W X Y Z

1 2 3 4 5 6 7 8 9 0

Unit 1

Manuscript and Slant Print

Lessons 1–30

Stroke Formations of Slant Print

a—oval, up, down
b—down, oval
c—small curve
d—oval, up, down
e—across, curve
f—curve, down, across
g—oval, up, down, curve
h—down, up, curve, down
i—down, dot
j—down, curve, dot
k—down, forward-slanting (f-s) line, backward-slanting (b-s) line
l—down
m—down, up, curve, down, up, curve, down
n—down, up, curve, down
o—small oval
p—down, up, oval
q—oval, up, down, curve
r—down, up, curve
s—curve, curve
t—down, across
u—down, curve, up, down
v—b-s line, f-s line
w—b-s line, f-s line, b-s line, f-s line
x—f-s line, b-s line
y—b-s line, f-s line
z—across, f-s line, across

A—f-s line, b-s line, across
B—down, across, curve, across; across, curve, across
C—large curve
D—down, across, curve, across
E—down, across, across, across
F—down, across, across
G—large curve, across
H—down, down, across
I—down, across, across
J—down, curve, across
K—down, f-s line, b-s line
L—down, across
M—down, b-s line, f-s line, down
N—down, b-s line, up
O—large oval
P—down, across, curve, across
Q—large oval, b-s line
R—down, across, curve, across, b-s line
S—curve, curve
T—down, across
U—down, curve, up
V—b-s line, f-s line
W—b-s line, f-s line, b-s line, f-s line
X—f-s line, b-s line
Y—b-s line, f-s line, down
Z—across, f-s line, across

Lesson 1
General Review of Manuscript Letters

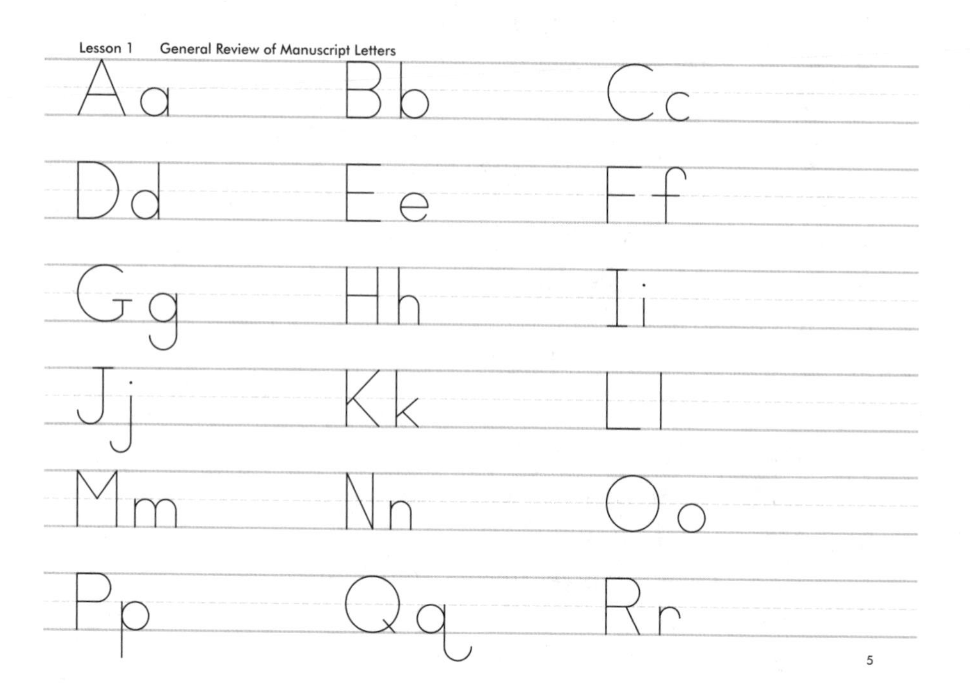

Aim of the Lesson

To review the forms of the letters of the manuscript alphabet.

Instructions for the Teacher

Begin the class period by **introducing the children to their books. Have them turn to this lesson. Explain that since they may have forgotten some of the letter forms** over the summer, they are going to see which one were forgotten and which ones they still remember.

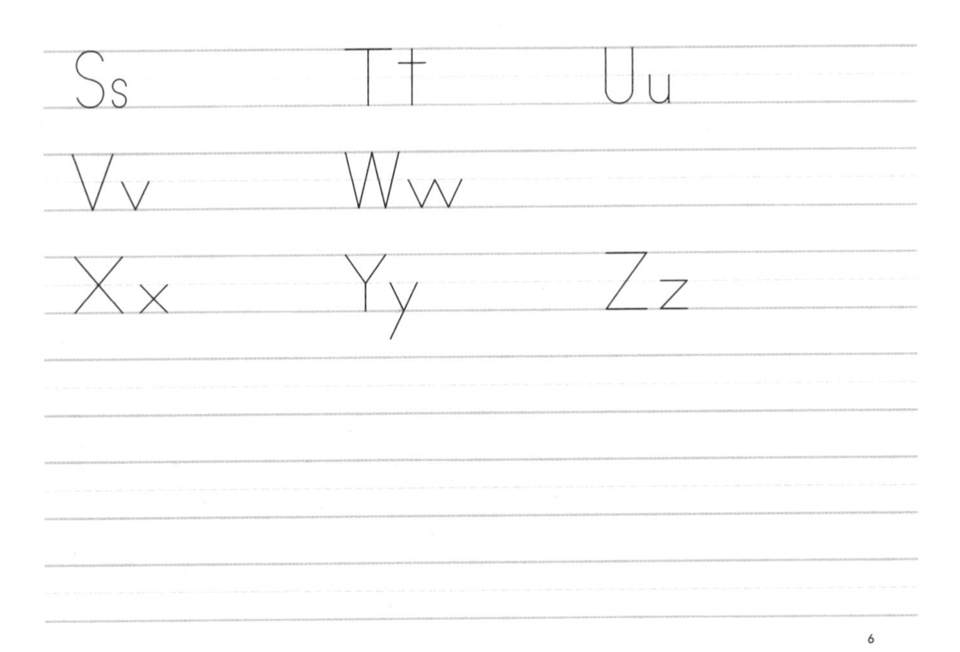

On the blackboard the children should print this sentence: "I will write as well as I can this year." Remind them to write their letters as neatly as they can **with proper spacing and alignment** (review these two terms with them).

*Back at their seats they should trace each letter in the lesson and then copy each form once in the space following. The space at the bottom of the second page is for practice of incorrectly formed letters.

Check on deterioration in the children's writing since last school year, if possible. You can be sure there will be some. Though they will likely remember basic letter shapes, some of the details may have been forgotten. You will need to remind them in some areas, such as making strokes within letters join correctly, making the points of the letters touch the lines above and below, and giving slanting lines the proper slant.

You may also need to mention correct posture if the children are sitting or standing incorrectly. This will be emphasized more in Lesson 2.

Lesson 2
Reducing Size

Lesson 2 Reducing Size

Jesus went about doing good.

He healed the sick and made

the blind see.

7

Aim of the Lesson

To help the children reduce their writing from the three-fourths-inch size to the one-half-inch size; to review the manuscript strokes.

Instructions for the Teacher

As you look at the lesson with the children, **call their attention to the size of the letters.** Explain that since they are making the letters smaller, **they should also bring the letters and words just a little bit closer together.**

At the blackboard the children should print the first sentence of the lesson, "Jesus went about going good." Then **have them print the manuscript strokes** as you call them out. These strokes are *down (|), across (—), forward-slanting (/), backward-slanting (\ ), circle (o), and curve (∪).*

Before the children begin work on the lesson, have them **describe proper posture** to you. Remind them to use it as they work their penmanship lesson. Also **remind them of correct habits for holding their pencils and placing their papers** as shown in the front of their books and in "Posture, Pencil Holding, and Paper Placement."

*At their seats the children should copy each line of writing twice in the spaces below. Beyond the dividing line in the middle of the last three lines, they should fill the space by printing the manuscript strokes.

Check areas of quality which the children may have forgotten from first grade penmanship. Remind them to make curves and circles as neatly as they can, straight lines as straight as possible, and slanted lines as nearly correct as possible. Their letters should also be well aligned at the top and bottom and in the middle. Their letters and words should be properly spaced.

You may need to emphasize the manuscript strokes, especially if you have students who did not have this course in writing last year. They should have at least enough acquaintance with the strokes to understand how they are used to make the manuscript letters.

Practice Sentences

1. God made all things in just six days.
2. God never tells a lie.
3. God was pleased with Abel.

Lesson 3
Writing Names

Lesson 3 Writing Names

Lester Miriam Paul Ida

Frank P. Jones Joy Adams

9

Aim of the Lesson

To teach the children principles of name writing both for their own names and for the names of others.

Instructions for the Teacher

As the children open their books to this lesson, discuss with them the fact that **each of us writes his name quite often.** We may write our names as often as four times a day, or more. **Do we write our names as neatly as we should,** or are we careless?

Write your name and middle initial on the blackboard.

Explain that an initial is only the first letter of a word or name with a period following. Even though there is a period after the letter, the middle initial and the last name are not spaced as far apart as two sentences would be. Remember, too, that **the middle initial must be capitalized, just like the first letter of each complete name.**

At the blackboard each child should write his name with its middle initial. Encourage them to write their names neatly and carefully. Remind them that they also ought to write their names neatly on all their papers.

*After reminding the children of their posture and pencil holding, have them proceed with the lesson. Have them copy the first and fourth rows twice in the rows immediately below. In the seventh, eighth, and ninth rows, they should practice writing their own names. Each should write his first name, his first and middle name together, his full name, his first and last name together, then his name with a middle initial. Show on the blackboard just how these should be arranged on the page.

Lesson 4
Stick Letters and Numerals

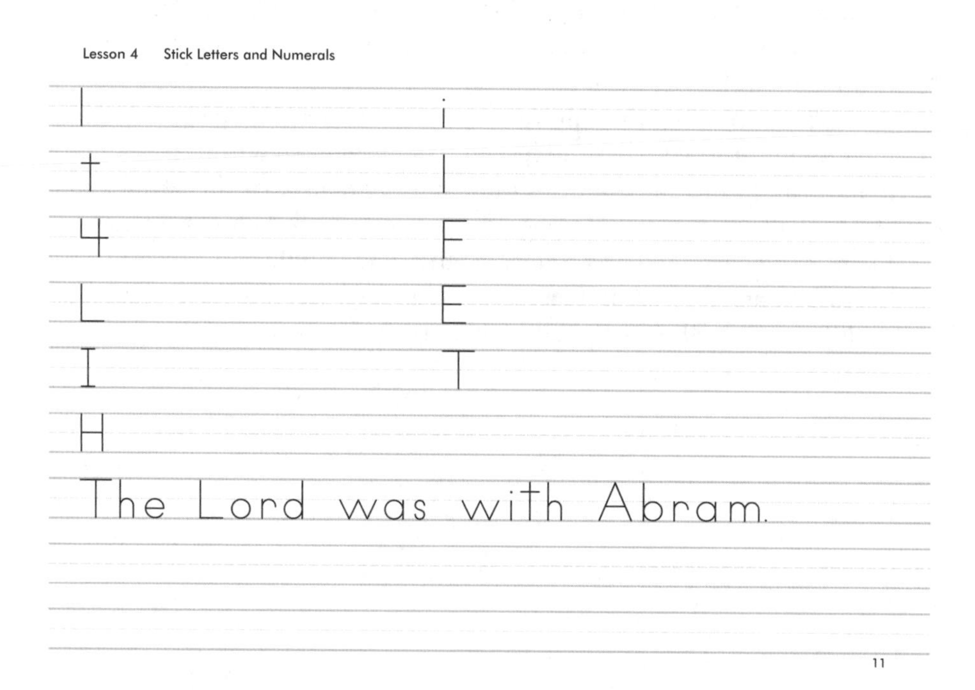

Aim of the Lesson

To refresh the children's memory on the formation of letters and numerals made with down and across lines.

Instructions for the Teacher

To begin with, **explain** to the children that **this lesson is a review of stick letters and numerals.**

In introducing the lesson, ask them if they remember **what kind of strokes compose stick letters.** The answer is **down lines (|) and across lines (—).** All of the letters in the first part of the lesson are made up of these two strokes. These have no curves, circles, or slanting lines.

Ask the children to tell you **what rules are important to remember when making stick letters.** You can remind them of these:

1. Down lines are made **from top to bottom** and across lines **from left to right.**
2. **The lines should be made as straight as possible,** without waves.
3. The lines should be **joined carefully so that they do not leave gaps or overlaps.**
4. The **down lines should not look like slanted lines.**

At the blackboard the children should first draw the two strokes which are used in these letters and numerals. Then have them draw the letter *t,* the numeral *4,* and the letter *E.*

*In the six upper rows of the lesson, the children should trace each letter and numeral, then copy each to the end of the space allotted. The sentence in row seven should be copied twice in the two rows below.

Insist that the children follow the four rules above for making stick letters. In the sentence be sure the children are **forming the letters correctly and spacing words and letters consistently.**

Practice Sentences

1. Of course, little Isaac grew.
2. Abram did not want to quarrel.
3. Lot chose the land that looked the best.

Lesson 5
Slant Letters and Numerals

Lesson 5 Slant Letters and Numerals

k v w

x y z

7 X A

N Z K

M Y V

W

Esau went out to kill a deer.

13

Aim of the Lesson

To refresh the children's memory on the formation of letters and numerals made with slanting lines.

Instructions for the Teacher

Begin by **discussing briefly** with the children **the kind of letters being practiced** in this lesson.

At the blackboard the children should draw the backward-slanting line (\ ) and the forward-slanting line (/). Work up a counting drill using the two strokes to give the children the feel of these slanting lines. The letter *x* would be good to use for this drill.

Discuss rules for making slant letters correctly. Here are some:

1. **The slanting lines are always made from top to bottom.**
2. **The lines should not be slanted too much or too little.** (Demonstrate correct and incorrect slants.)
3. **Each slanting line should join or cross other lines accurately and at the right places.** (Demonstrate.)
4. **Slanting lines should not be wavy.**

Discuss the meaning of alignment. Remind the children that their letters should just touch the lines, but not go beyond them. Give a brief demonstration.

*At their seats the children should proceed with the lesson. They should trace each letter, then copy it in the space allotted. The sentence should be copied twice in the two rows below.

Check the children's work to **be sure the slant lines are correctly slanted.** Also check to see how well the children are **adjusting to the decreased letter size.** Look for things such as extra-wide letters and spaces, and letters going over the lines. Also be sure the children are **maintaining proper posture** and are **holding their pencils right.**

Lesson 6
Circle Letters and Numerals

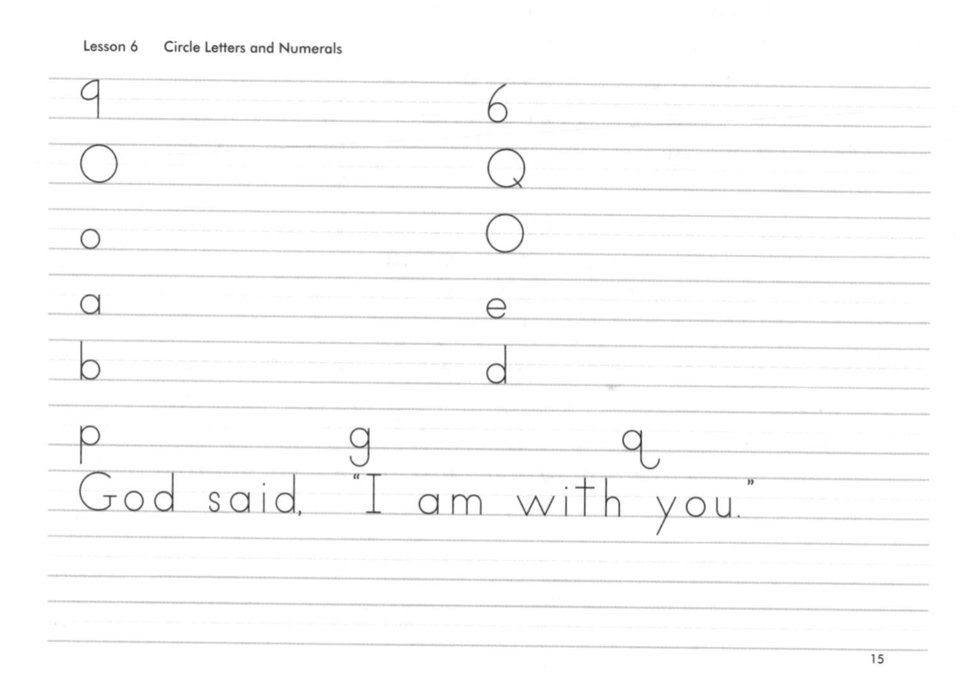
Lesson 6 Circle Letters and Numerals

9 6

O Q

o O

a e

b d

p g q

God said, "I am with you."

15

Aim of the Lesson

To refresh the children's memory on the formation of letters and numerals made with circles.

Instructions for the Teacher

Introduce the lesson, explaining what kind of letters are being practiced in this lesson.

Discuss the formation of the circle stroke (O), especially as it is used in these letters. **Have the children give you some of the important things to remember when making the circle stroke.**

Following are a few:

1. The circle stroke should **begin on the upper right side,** not at the top. This helps to avoid a point where the ends meet.
2. The circles should be made **as nearly round as possible.**
3. **Circles can be drawn more neatly if they are drawn quickly.** If we stop while drawing to see how we are coming along, we will likely make a point or wave in the line.
4. We should **be careful in joining a circle to a down line,** so that there is no gap or overlap, but that the lines just touch.

At the blackboard the children should draw a number of large and small circles.

*At their seats the children should proceed with the lesson. They should trace each letter, then copy it in the space allotted. The sentence should be copied twice on the lines below.

Draw the children's attention to the **quotation marks** around "I am with you." Explain how quotation marks are made, and that they are placed around the exact words that someone has said.

Watch the formation of circles in the sentence as well as in the letters in the upper part. Work at obtaining as nearly accurate circle formation as possible.

Practice Sentences

1. Jacob got up early in the morning.
2. The Lord is in this place.
3. Jacob worked seven years for Rachel.

Lesson 7
Curve Letters and Numerals

Lesson 7 Curve Letters and Numerals

2 3 5

8 C G

S D P

R B J

U c u

r n m

h f j s

Jacob asked God to help him.

17

Aim of the Lesson

To refresh the children's memory on the formation of letters made with curve lines, with special emphasis on teaching them how curves are different in different letters.

Instructions for the Teacher

Place a curve on the board and discuss it. Ask the children what they remember about curve lines from first grade. After some discussion, **remind them that not all curves are the same. They are not always of the same size or in the same position.**

Although they are frequently half-circles, this is not always the case. Some are almost whole circles. **Compare** *3, 5, C, c, n,* **and** *j.* **Show how the curve is different for each letter and numeral.** Yet each one has the characteristic of a curve, which is being a part circle. If the children remember that the curve is part of a circle, it will help them to make a better-shaped curve.

At the blackboard the children should practice several of the curve letters.

*At their seats they should trace each letter and numeral in the first seven rows, then copy each in the space allotted. The sentence should be copied once in the last row.

As you evaluate, **watch for sharp points and irregularities in the children's curves.** If you see a child's curves having any irregularities that noticeably affect the neatness or legibility of the letter, call his attention to it. Have him practice the letter until you can see definite improvement.

Lesson 8
Finding Mistakes

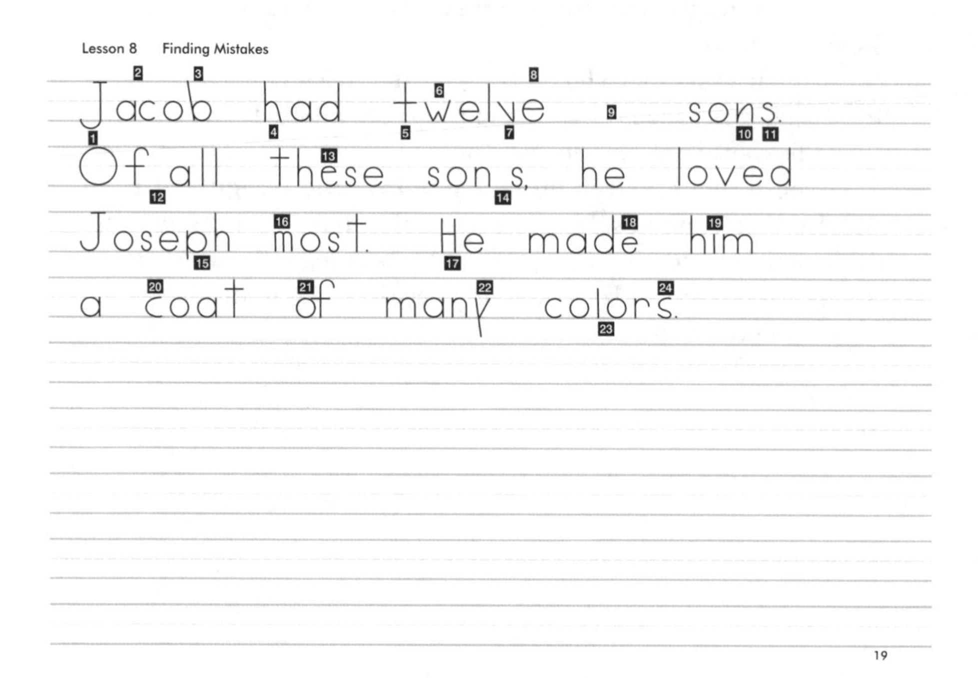

Answer Key

- **1**—below line
- **2**—too close
- **3**—slanted
- **4**—slanted
- **5**—cross too low
- **6**—poorly formed
- **7**—poor slant
- **8**—too high
- **9**—too much space
- **10**—poorly formed
- **11**—poorly formed
- **12**—too close
- **13**—poorly formed
- **14**—too far apart
- **15**—too short
- **16**—too narrow
- **17**—too small
- **18**—too small

19—no dot
20—poorly formed
21—too close
22—poorly formed
23—too short
24—poorly formed

Aim of the Lesson

To teach the children to identify errors in writing as a means of helping them see errors in their own writing.

Instructions for the Teacher

Look with the children at the lesson. **Explain that they are to look over these three sentences and find all the errors there that they can. There are twenty-four** altogether. Some of the errors are spacing errors, some are alignment errors, some are height errors, and some are letter-formation errors.

*Instruct the children to look well at each letter and word and the spaces between the letters and words to be sure they are finding all the mistakes. **Have them draw short arrows pointing to each mistake.** Show them what they are to do by looking together at the errors in the word *Jacob*. When they have finished finding the errors in the three sentences, **have them copy the sentences in the lines below.** They should correct each error and be sure they are not making any new errors. In the last line they should print the six manuscript strokes (| – \ / O ◡).

In this lesson the children will need to look at writing from the evaluation angle instead of from the writing angle. **It may help them to see some mistakes they may be regularly making.** Help the children find any mistakes which they did not catch. Be sure they have found all the errors in the sentences before they begin to copy them. Also be sure each child is sitting up straight and holding his pencil correctly.

Practice Sentences

1. They put Joseph into a pit.
2. Jacob thought his son was dead.
3. The keeper of the prison liked Joseph.

Lesson 9
How Strokes and Letters Change With Slant

There will be seven good years.

| = /

\ = |

/ = /

O = O

o = o

◠◡ = ◠◡

— = —

Aim of the Lesson

To introduce principles of slant print to the children.

Instructions for the Teacher

Have the children open their books to this lesson and look at the sentence at the top of the page. Explain to them that the kind of writing in this sentence is called slant print. Learning this kind of printing now will help in learning cursive writing later this year.

At the blackboard demonstrate each stroke and discuss how it changes in slant print. Explain to the children that each of the three straight strokes is slanted farther forward. The circles are made more narrow and slanted forward and are called ovals rather than circles. The curves in slant print are part ovals just as regular curves are part circles. The across line remains the same both in regular and slant print.

Send the children to the blackboard and have them practice these strokes a number of times to get the feel of them.

With the children at their seats, **show them how they are to place their papers when they print slant print.** Their papers should be slanted about the same as is normal for cursive writing (see "Posture, Pencil Holding, and Paper Placement"). **Be especially sure that left-handers have their papers slanted correctly** (See "Special Instructions for Left-handed Pupils").

*In rows three through nine, the children should copy the second stroke in each row to the end of the row. When they have done this, have them copy the sentence in row one the best they can in the row immediately below.

Although not all penmanship courses teach slant print, we feel that if it is taught correctly, it can be an important help in learning cursive writing. Learning **slant print gives the children a sense of progress in their ability,** without the confusion that would result from an immediate changeover to cursive writing. It is also a relaxing form of printing and, once learned, will likely be used by the children for the rest of their lives.

This lesson is slant print in a nutshell; therefore, **do not expect the children's writing to be perfect at this point.** The next twenty or so lessons will elaborate on the principles introduced here.

As the teacher, you should realize that **it is actually the slant of the paper that determines the slant of the writing.** A paper which is straight up-and-down, because of the natural movement of the hand and fingers, will produce vertical writing. But if the paper is slanted about 30 degrees (top to left for right-handers, top to right for left-handers), the natural movements of the hand will produce correctly slanted writing. Therefore, one of the most important things for you to emphasize in teaching slant print is that the paper be correctly slanted.

Lesson 10
Stick Letters in Slant

Lesson 10 Stick Letters in Slant

l i t

L F E

I T H

l

lit till little Hill tilt

Joseph was ruler over the land.

23

Aim of the Lesson

To teach the children how to form the stick letters properly in slant.

Instructions for the Teacher

Explain to the children that the letters in this lesson are the same as those in Lesson 4. Ask the children **what kind of strokes make up stick letters.** The answer is **down lines and across lines.** So, to write stick letters in slant print, we will need to know how to make down lines and across lines in slant. In Lesson 9 we learned that **the across line does not change.** We also learned that **the down line,** which is straight up-and-down in regular print, **is slanted forward** to make the writing slanted. **Have the children look at the slanting down line** in row four to see just how much it slants. **You may also want to demonstrate proper slant** at the blackboard.

At the blackboard the children should draw the slanted down line correctly a number of times. Also **call out several of the letters from this lesson, and see if the children can figure out how to draw them in slant print** on the board. **Be sure the children realize how the slanted down line affects each letter.**

*At their seats the children should proceed with the lesson. In the first three rows, they should trace each letter, then copy each one in the space allotted. They should fill rows four and five with copies of the slanted down line. Row six should be copied in row seven, and row eight in row nine (note that row eight is regular manuscript).

In this lesson, **work to perfect the slanted down line.** Teach the children to form the line accurately and consistently. This will take practice.

Up through Lesson 13, the children should use regular manuscript writing for their daily lessons. From Lesson 14 on, they should use slant print.

Practice Sentences

1. Joseph gathered much food.
2. A great famine came.
3. Joseph knew his brothers.

Lesson 11
Slant Letters in Slant

Lesson 11 Slant Letters in Slant

k v w

x x y z

X X A N N

Z K M M

Y V V W W

Israel got ready to move.

25

Aim of the Lesson

To teach the children how to form the slant letters properly in slant.

Instructions for the Teacher

Remind the children that **the letters in this lesson are the same letters which were reviewed earlier** in Lesson 5, only this time they are in slant rather than in regular manuscript. Some of them also have changes in the way they are made; these are demonstrated for the children.

Describe the change which takes place in changing slanting

lines from regular to slant print. Explain that the **backward-slanting line** is still slanted backward, but not so much as it is in regular print. It is almost straight up-and-down. **Demonstrate** this stroke on the blackboard several times.

The **forward-slanting line** is slanted more than the regular forward-slanting line. **Demonstrate** this stroke also on the blackboard.

Show how these two strokes are actually used in letters, using the letters *k, v,* and *M.* **Be sure to use the new order and direction of some strokes** as shown on the students' page. These changes have been made to accommodate the greater speed with which slant print is written.

Have the children practice the two strokes on the board, and one or two of the letters, before proceeding with the lesson.

*In row one, the children should copy the slant backward-slanting line and the slant forward-slanting line in the space following these strokes. In rows two through six, the children should trace each letter and copy it in the space following. In row seven, they should copy the slanted down line to the end of the row. Row eight should be copied in row nine. **Be sure the children change the slant of their papers to straight up-and-down for the last line.**

Check the children's **posture,** and be sure they are **sitting up straight with their feet on the floor.**

Help the children learn to use the natural movement of their hands to form slant letters. Remember, printing slanted *is* natural if the paper is correctly slanted.

Since the children have three degrees of slant to make correctly in the slanting letters (down line, forward-slanting line, backward-slanting line), **they will probably find this lesson difficult.** Therefore, give them plenty of practice, using the back of the page and other paper as necessary.

Lesson 12
Circle Letters in Slant (Oval Letters)

Lesson 12 Circle Letters in Slant (Oval Letters)

O o
o a a
e b
d d p p
g g q q
O Q
\ /
pad dog bib bed pig gap

27

Aim of the Lesson

To teach the children how to form the circle letters properly in slant, noting especially that the oval replaces the circle.

Instructions for the Teacher

Compare the letters in this lesson with the same letters which were reviewed in Lesson 6. Explain to the children again that **the shape we use to form the circle letters in slant print is called**

an oval, not a circle. So in slant print we will begin calling them oval letters rather than circle letters. On the blackboard, again **compare the shape** of the oval and the circle. Show distinctly that **the oval is narrower than the circle** and that **it slants forward.**

Have the children form a number of ovals in the air. Then send them to the blackboard to draw one. Have them draw around that oval rapidly a number of times, trying to stay on the lines each time. This will help them to get the feel of the oval stroke. Since the oval is one of the basic strokes in cursive writing, it will be valuable for your children to learn this stroke now.

At their seats the children should look at the letters in the lesson. **Ask them to tell you which letter does not have a complete oval in it.** The answer is **the letter** *e*. It has **almost** a complete oval in it, but not quite. You may need to give special help to your children with this letter. Also, since the slant letter *e* is made slightly faster than the manuscript, be sure they maintain a distinct point on it (e, not e).

In this lesson again there are some changes in the way some of the letters are made. **Be sure that the children understand these changes.** They should make the slant print *a, b, d, p, g,* and *q* **without lifting their pencils.** This is done because slant print is written faster than manuscript. Also, the children are preparing for cursive writing, in which whole words are written without the pencil being lifted.

*In row one, the children should trace around the printed ovals several times, then copy them in the space following each one. In rows two through six, they should trace each letter and copy it in the space immediately following. In row seven, which is a review of the slant backward-slanting and forward-slanting lines, the children should trace each stroke, then copy it in the space allotted. The words in row eight should be copied in row nine directly below.

Again be sure the children are slanting their papers correctly and holding their arms correctly so that natural hand movement can help them in forming slant strokes.

Practice Sentences

1. The poor brothers felt very sad.
2. Satan is the enemy of God.
3. Job had a big family.

Lesson 13
Curve Letters in Slant

Lesson 13 Curve Letters in Slant

O ⌒ ∪ o ⌒ ∪

c u r

n m h

f j s

C D G

B J P

R S U

Job had three friends.

29

Aim of the Lesson

To teach the children how to form the curve letters in slant.

Instructions for the Teacher

Compare the slant curves with the oval, using row one as a guide. Draw an oval **on the blackboard.** Show that the slant curves are made from an oval, just like regular curves are made from a circle. The children should remember this fact when they print slant curves.

Have the children come to the blackboard and practice the oval by drawing one, then tracing over it rapidly several times,

as in the last lesson. Then **have them draw a number of both kinds of slant curves. They should also draw some slanted down lines** as review.

*At their seats the children should proceed with the lesson. In row one, they should copy both the large and the small slant curves, alternating the upper and lower forms on the line. In rows two through seven, the children should trace each letter and copy it in the space following. The sentence in row eight is to be copied in row nine.

You may need to **give your children special help with some of the capital letters,** such as *B, D, P,* and *R.* In these letters the curves are in a sideways position with across lines attached on each end; **they may be slightly confusing.**

Be sure the children's papers are slanted correctly. Also be sure that they are doing their best to make their slants accurate.

Beginning with the next lesson, the children should use slant print for all of their writing.

Lesson 14
Numerals in Slant

Lesson 14 Numerals in Slant

0 1

2 3

4 5

6 7

8 9

Moses was put into a

little boat by his mother.

31

Aim of the Lesson

To teach the children how to form the numerals in slant.

Instructions for the Teacher

Give the children a quick review of the slant strokes. Send them to the blackboard, and have them draw each slant stroke carefully as you call out the names (down, forward-slanting, backward-slanting, across, oval, curve). Help them make each stroke correctly.

Following blackboard drill, have the children look at the numerals in the lesson. **Explain to them that the same basic principles apply**

to slant numerals as apply to slant letters. After **demonstrating the strokes that compose each numeral,** have the children proceed with the lesson.

*In rows one through five, the children should trace each numeral and copy it in the space following. They should also copy the sentence in rows six and eight, in rows seven and nine.

Again be sure the children are slanting their papers correctly. Devote some attention to **helping the children use the correct slant in forming the down, backward-slanting, and forward-slanting lines in slant print.** They already have a general idea of correct slant for these three lines, yet they may still seem somewhat unsure. The best way for you to help them is to **evaluate and correct the slant of these lines while they are writing them. Also give the children help in forming ovals and curves** as you see they need it.

Practice Sentences

1. God had a plan for Moses.
2. Moses was hid three months.
3. The king was afraid of Israel.

Lesson 15
A and *E* in Slant

Lesson 15 A and *E* in Slant

A

a

E

e

God told Moses to go back

to the land of Egypt.

33

Aim of the Lesson

To teach the formation of the small and capital letters *A* and *E* in slant.

Instructions for the Teacher

The important thing in this lesson is to **help the children learn to form in slant print the four letter forms taught here. Tie in an ongoing review of slant print strokes** in this lesson and the next twelve lessons as you help the children form the slant print letters of the alphabet.

In this lesson, when teaching capital letters *A* and *E,* **you have an opportunity to stress the down, backward-slanting, and forward-slanting lines.** These slants may still be difficult for the children.

Place the four letters on the blackboard as the children watch. Explain the strokes for each letter as you do so. Then **have the children come to the blackboard and print the letters** a number of times while you help them with formation.

The formation of the letter *e* **deserves special attention.** Show the children that, at the end of the across line, the curve actually goes **forward** just a bit before curving around toward the back of the letter. Remind them again to keep a "corner" on the front of their *e*'s.

*At their seats the children should proceed with the lesson. In rows one through four, the children should trace each letter, then copy it to the end of the row. The sentence in rows five and seven should be copied in rows six and eight. The final row may be used for practice of whatever slant stroke or letter you feel the children need to practice.

While the main emphasis in these lessons is form, **you should not neglect other areas of quality. Alignment and spacing especially** should receive attention.

Be sure the children are **slanting their papers correctly** and are **exercising good posture.**

The stroke compositions of *A* and *E* are as follows: *A*—forward-slanting (f-s) line, backward-slanting (b-s) line, across; *a*—oval, up, down; *E*—down, across, across, across; *e*—across, curve.

Lesson 16
I and X in Slant

Lesson 16 *I* and *X* in Slant

I

i

X

x

The king would not give

the people straw.

35

Aim of the Lesson

To teach the formation of the small and capital *I* and *X* in slant.

Instructions for the Teacher

Demonstrate the letters *I* **and** *X* **in slant print with their small and capital forms** on the blackboard, **explaining the composition of each one in terms of strokes used in its formation.** Explain that the formation of these letters is basically very simple. Both forms of *I* are basically down lines, and both forms of *X* are slanting lines, one forward and one backward. Capital *I* contains two short across lines at the top and bottom, and small *i* has a dot.

With the letter *X,* you will need to remind the children that the strokes should cross each other exactly in the middle.

On the blackboard the children should practice these letter forms in slant print. Help them with formation where necessary.

*The children should trace over and copy the letters in rows one through four in slant print to the end of the rows. The sentence in rows five and seven should be copied in rows six and eight. Row nine can be used by the children to practice the four forms of the letters *A* and *E* from the last lesson.

Remember that you are to be emphasizing the strokes of slant print, not just the letters. The slanted down line will be carried over later into cursive writing in exactly the same form. So whatever practice they get in writing this stroke will not be wasted effort.

Here are the stroke formations of *I* and *X: I*—down, across, across; *i*—down, dot; *X* and *x*—f-s line, b-s line.

Practice Sentences

1. God told Moses to talk to the king.
2. Aaron's rod became a snake.
3. The water was turned into blood.

Lesson 17
U and *Y* in Slant

Lesson 17 *U and Y in Slant*

U

u

Y

y

The flies were gone, but the

king did not let Israel go.

37

Aim of the Lesson

To teach the formation of the small and capital letters *U* and *Y* in slant.

Instructions for the Teacher

On the blackboard demonstrate the bottom curve as it is formed in the letter *U*. **Show the children again how this curve is formed from the oval. Print the four letter forms on the blackboard, explaining the stroke formation of each letter.** Help the children to join all the strokes of *Y* accurately. Also help them to join the curves with the down lines smoothly in both forms of the letter *U*.

Send the children to the blackboard and have them practice the two sizes of bottom curves, then both forms of the letters *U* and *Y*.

*In rows one through four, the children should trace each letter form and then copy it to the end of the row. The sentence in rows five and seven should be copied in rows six and eight. Row nine should be used to practice the four forms (small and capital) of the letters *I* and *X*.

In the sentence, **be sure the children are learning to move their writing along smoothly and evenly** with correct spacing and consistent slant. **Help the children remember to slant their papers correctly.** Remind them of this frequently, as it is all-important for neat slant print or cursive writing.

The stroke combinations for *U* and *Y* are as follows: *U*—down, curve, up; *u*—down, curve, up, down; *Y*—b-s line, f-s line, down; *y*—b-s line, f-s line.

Lesson 18
B and *D* in Slant

Lesson 18 *B and D in Slant*

B

b

D

d

Hail from God broke down

the trees in Egypt.

39

Aim of the Lesson

To teach the formation of the small and capital letters *B* and *D* in slant.

Instructions for the Teacher

In this lesson the **capitals *B* and *D* have side curves. Explain to the children how side curves are formed from ovals** in the same manner as bottom and top curves are. Instead of being taken from the top or bottom of an oval, they are taken from the side ( ).

Demonstrate how the capital letters *B* and *D* are made from

down lines, across lines, and side curves. In the demonstration, **also show the children that they need to bring the curve in farther at the bottom than at the top** in order to make the letter slant as it should (correct: **B** ; incorrect: **B**).

When you explain the letters *B* and *D*, **emphasize making each loop,** which consists of two across lines and a curve, **as one movement.** Rather than thinking in terms of three separate strokes for each, have the children begin thinking of them as curves with extensions on each end. **This will help them make these loops smoothly.**

Also demonstrate the small letters *b* **and** *d*. Remind the children that these letters are simply backward from each other.

Have the children practice these four letter forms on the blackboard several times. **Assist them with letter formation and accuracy.** Help them especially with their capital *B*'s and *D*'s.

*At their seats the children should proceed with the lesson by tracing the letters in rows one through four and then copying them to the end of the rows. The sentence in rows five and seven should be copied in rows six and eight. Row nine should be used to practice the letters *U* and *Y*.

The stroke formations for *B* and *D* are as follows: *B*—down, across, curve, across, across, curve, across; *b*—down, oval; *D*—down, across, curve, across; *d*—oval, up, down.

Practice Sentences

1. God sent darkness to Egypt.
2. God made the king's heart hard.
3. Locusts and hail spoiled all the crops.

Lesson 19
C and *G* in Slant

Lesson 19 C and G in Slant

C

c

G

g

God told His people to put

blood around their doors.

41

Aim of the Lesson

To teach the formation of the small and capital letters *C* and *G* in slant.

Instructions for the Teacher

This lesson should revolve around the formation of the oval. Each form of both *C* and *G* contains either a full or part oval. **On the blackboard the children should draw a number of large ovals rapidly, retracing each stroke** a number of times. **Demonstrate each letter form, then have the children practice** each themselves.

The two forms of the letter *C* are quite simple. Both are curves, about three-fourths of a complete oval. The distance that each line extends from the top line down is the same as it extends from the bottom line up. **Capital letter *G* is somewhat different in slant print** from regular manuscript. **Rather than an up line being drawn** at the end of the curve, as in regular manuscript, **the oval is just extended farther before an across line is placed at the top. This makes slant print *G* a two-stroke rather than a three-stroke letter.** With the small letter *g,* you will want to be sure the children's formation of the bottom curve makes it a true slant curve.

*At their seats the children should proceed with the lesson. In rows one through four, they should trace over each letter form, then copy it in the space following. The sentence in rows five and seven should be copied in rows six and eight. Row nine should be used to practice the four forms of the letters *B* and *D.*

In the sentence, help the children with spacing and letter formation if necessary. **Be particular on letter forms which the children have studied in detail in the past few lessons,** such as *a, e, b,* and *d.* The children should also do their best in the review line.

The stroke combinations for *C* and *G* are as follows: *C*—large curve; *c*—small curve; *G*—large curve, across; *g*—oval, up, down, curve.

Lesson 20
F and *H* in Slant

Lesson 20 *F and H in Slant*

F

f

H

h

He had a pillar of fire for

them to follow at night.

43

Aim of the Lesson

To teach the formation of the small and capital letters *F* and *H* in slant.

Instructions for the Teacher

Explain that **the key strokes used in the formation of the letters *F* and *H* are the down line, the across line, and the curve.** The curve this time is a top curve for both the small letter *f* and the small letter *h*. **On the blackboard demonstrate how a top curve is taken from an oval.**

Have the children go to the blackboard and draw several

ovals, then a number of small top curves. Help them carry the oval feel into their curves. **Be sure their curves are oval-style curves rather than circle-style curves.** Oval-style top curves have more of a point at the top toward the front, whereas circle-style curves are evenly rounded all the way.

Be sure the children are beginning the small letter ***f*** **far enough forward** so that the end of the down line does not come too close to the previous letter.

With all the letters, be sure they are joining the strokes neatly without gaps or overlaps and are putting correct slant into each letter.

With the children at their seats, **ensure that their papers are correctly slanted, their posture is correct, and their pencils are held right** before they begin the lesson.

*In rows one through four, they should trace over each letter, then copy it to the end of the row. The sentences in rows five and seven should be copied in rows six and eight. In row nine they should practice the four forms of the letters *C* and *G*.

The stroke combinations for *F* and *H* are: *F*—down, across, across; *f*—curve, down across; *H*—down, down across; *h*—down, up, curve, down.

Practice Sentences

1. Egypt chased the children of Israel.
2. Their chariot wheels fell off.
3. Israel sang a song to God.

Lesson 21
J and *K* in Slant

Lesson 21 J and K in Slant

J

j

K

k

They told Moses to give

them water to drink.

45

Aim of the Lesson

To teach the formation of the small and capital letters *J* and *K* in slant.

Instructions for the Teacher

Have the children look at the letters *J* and *K* in their books and also identify the strokes which they see in these letters.

Draw the letters on the blackboard, and explain their formation as you do so. **Pay special attention to the forms of the letter *K*. Demonstrate carefully where each line touches another**

line, and the proper amount of slant for each line. Show that one should be able to draw a slanted down line along the right side of both forms of the letter *K*, touching the ends of the two slanting lines and having the same slant as the first stroke of the letter (*K*).

Give the children a brief warmup at the blackboard **by having them print the slanted down, forward-slanting, and backward-slanting lines** several times. Next **have them print both forms of the letters *J* and *K* in slant print** a number of times. **Be sure the curves on the bottom of *J* are oval-style** rather than circle-style curves. Also **be sure the children are joining the strokes of both forms of the letter *K* properly** at the right places **and are putting the right amount of slant** in each down, forward-slanting, and backward-slanting line.

When the children have gone back to their seats and are ready to begin the lesson, pause a moment to **be sure they are exercising proper posture and correct pencil-holding habits.**

*In rows one through four, the children should trace each letter, then copy it to the end of the row. The sentence in rows five and seven should be copied in rows six and eight. In row nine they should practice the four forms of the letters *F* and *H*.

The stroke combinations for *J* and *K are: J*—down, curve, across; *j—down, curve, dot; K* and *k*—down, f-s line, b-s line.

Lesson 22
T and *L* in Slant

Lesson 22 *T* and *L* in Slant

T

t

L

l

The Lord was angry when

the people bowed to a calf.

47

Aim of the Lesson

To teach the formation of the small and capital letters *T* and *L* in slant.

Instructions for the Teacher

Explain to the children that the letters *T* and *L* are very simple letters to form in slant print, as they also are in regular printing. However, **there are a few things they need to remember if they want to make these letters correctly. Have the children name some of these, such as:** the across lines in *L* and *T* must be made the right length; the cross in the *t* should be the right distance up from the middle line; and the down lines must have the right amount of slant.

The children should not need a lot of demonstration with these letters because of their simplicity. **Have them come to the blackboard and first draw some ordinary down lines and across lines in slant, then the four forms of these two letters several times. Check the children's work** in the areas of form and quality mentioned in the preceding paragraph.

With the children at their seats, **emphasize again the point of being sure the across line on the letter *t* crosses at the right place. Also be sure the children make the top and bottom of each down line touch the top and bottom lines.** After you are certain the children are not being careless with their posture, have them proceed with the lesson.

*The children should trace each letter in rows one through four, then copy it to the end of the row. The sentence in rows five and seven should be copied in rows six and eight. In row nine they should practice the four forms of the letters *J* and *K*.

The stroke combinations for *T* and *L* are: *T* and *t*—down, across; *L*—down, across; *l*—down.

Practice Sentences

1. Honor thy father and mother.
2. Remember the Sabbath Day.
3. Thou shalt not steal.

Lesson 23
M and *N* in Slant

Lesson 23 M and N in Slant

M

m

N

n

God told Moses how His

house was to be made.

49

Aim of the Lesson

To teach the formation of the small and capital letters *M* and *N* in slant.

Instructions for the Teacher

As a quick review, have the children go to the blackboard and print the small and capital forms of the letters *A* **through** *L* **in slant print.** Then **look with them at the slant forms of the letters** *M* **and** *N*, both small and capital, keeping in mind the following points for explanation.

Explain that **with the capital letter *M* the backward-slanting line and the forward-slanting line must meet halfway between the two down lines.** Explain that **it is important to make the point at the bottom of the two slanting strokes right at the middle line** rather than above or below it.

The curves of the small *m* and *n* should be smoothly rounded, with their **tops just touching the middle line.**

With capital *N* the children should make their **backward-slanting line and up stroke rapidly enough** to avoid a wavy appearance. The strokes of both capital *N* and *M* should be carefully joined.

Have the children draw several of each form of *M* and *N*, then send them back to their seats and **have them proceed with the lesson** under your supervision.

*In rows one through four, the children should trace the four forms of the letters *M* and *N* and copy each to the end of the row. The sentence in rows five and seven should be copied in rows six and eight. Row nine should be used to practice the letters *T* and *L*.

The stroke combinations for *M* and *N* are: *M*—down, b-s line, f-s line, down; *m*—down, up, curve, down, up, curve, down; *N*—down, b-s line, up; *n*—down, up, curve, down.

Lesson 24
O and *Q* in Slant

Lesson 24 O and Q in Slant

O

o

Q

q

One time God sent twelve

men to spy out Canaan.

51

Aim of the Lesson

To teach the formation of the small and capital letters *O* and *Q* in slant.

Instructions for the Teacher

At the blackboard your children should practice drawing small and large ovals. Have them trace around each oval a number of times before going on to form the next one.

When they have finished drawing as many ovals as you ask them to, **remind them that the ovals they have drawn are the two**

forms of the letter *O* and are also contained in the two forms of the letter *Q*.

Draw the two forms of the letter *Q* on the board, explaining briefly their formation. Remind the children that small *q* is just like *g*, except the curve is slightly smaller and goes in the opposite direction from the letter *g*'s curve.

Have the children draw these letters on the blackboard, helping them to print the ovals accurately. The ovals for each letter should have the same amount of roundness and the same amount of slant. Ovals should also be smoothly drawn without points at any place, not even at the top and bottom where the curve is sharper. It should still be rounded.

*Have the children trace the four forms of the letters *O* and *Q* and copy each to the end of the row. The sentence in rows five and seven should be copied in rows six and eight. In row nine, the children should review the letters *M* and *N*.

In the sentence, help the children with their spacing, reminding them to place the words and letters neither too far apart nor too close together.

The stroke combinations for *O* and *Q* are: *O* and *o*—oval; *Q*—oval, b-s line; *q*—oval, up, down, curve.

Practice Sentences

1. God wrote the Ten Commandments on two pieces of stone.
2. The tribe of Levi took care of the house of God.
3. Miriam found fault with her brother Moses.

Lesson 25
P and *R* in Slant

Lesson 25 *P* and *R* in Slant

P

p

R

r

God said no, but the

people still tried to go.

53

Aim of the Lesson

To teach the formation of the small and capital letters *P* and *R* in slant.

Instructions for the Teacher

Have the children identify the strokes for the capital letters *P* and *R*. Show them that the two are very much alike with only one difference. **The letter *R* contains an extra stroke, a backward-slanting line. After you have demonstrated** these two letters, **have the children come to the blackboard and practice them.**

Remind the children to make the two across lines blend smoothly with the curve. Also, the curve is an oval-style curve and should be made that way. The bottom end of the curve should come in somewhat farther than the top end, so that the across lines can be of equal length, and the letter can have a better appearance.

Small *p* and small *r* should also have oval-type curves. You should constantly beware lest your children try to make their curves regular circle style when printing slant print. However, the oval is a natural stroke in slant print, so you will not likely have problems unless a child tries to make the curve or circle with the regular vertical style. **Have the children practice these two small forms on the blackboard.**

Encourage the children to watch their alignment as they work the lesson. They should be sure their letters are touching the right lines at the right places.

*At their seats the children should proceed with the lesson. In rows one through four, they should trace each letter and copy it to the end of the row. The sentence in rows five and seven should be copied in rows six and eight. Row nine should be used to review and practice the letters *O* and *Q*.

The strokes for *P* and *R* are: *P*—down, across, curve, across; *p*—down, up, oval; *R*—down, across, curve, across, b-s line; *r*—down, up, curve.

Lesson 26
S and *Z* in Slant

Lesson 26 *S* and *Z* in Slant

S

s

Z

z

"Speak to the rock," God

told Moses.

55

Aim of the Lesson

To teach the formation of the small and capital letters *S* and *Z* in slant.

Instructions for the Teacher

Explain to the children that today they are going to learn the letters *S* and *Z* in slant print. **Draw the letter *S* on the blackboard,** showing that it is a double curve that is slanted. **Have the children come to the blackboard and draw a number of both forms of the letter *S*. Help them to make double curves smoothly and**

neatly, with each part of the double curve blending into the other part well. Since *S* is basically a double curve, **the key to making a good letter *S,* whether small or capital, lies in being able to make a smooth double curve.**

Getting the slant correct may also be somewhat difficult with the letter *S,* so you may need to give your children some special help with this. It may help to **draw sets of two slanted parallel lines the right distance apart,** so that the children can draw their letter *S*'s within them.

The letter *Z* is not difficult to form, although there are a few things to remember with both forms of the letter. One is that **with a slanting letter *Z,* the two across lines are offset**—the bottom across line lies somewhat to the left of the top across line. This happens because the forward-slanting line is more slanted in slant print than in regular manuscript.

Have the children practice drawing both forms of the letter *Z* on the blackboard.

*In rows one through four, the children should trace the four forms of *S* and *Z* and copy each to the end of the row. The sentence in rows five and seven should be copied in rows six and eight. Row nine should be used to practice and review the letters *P* and *R.*

The children may not have had much experience with the use of quotation marks. Since this is penmanship and not English, simply tell the children that they show when someone is speaking, without a lot of other explanation about them.

The strokes for *S* and *Z* are: *S* and *s*—curve, curve; *Z* and *z*—across, f-s line, across.

Practice Sentences

1. Aaron's rod was blooming.
2. Miriam died in the wilderness.
3. The people grumbled for bread to eat.

Lesson 27
V and *W* in Slant

Lesson 27 *V* and *W* in Slant

V

v

W

w

When Moses was about to die,

he saw the land of Canaan.

57

Aim of the Lesson

To teach the formation of the small and capital letters *V* and *W* in slant.

Instructions for the Teacher

Demonstrate and explain the stroke formation of the letters *V* and *W*. Have the children tell you how the letters *V* and *W* are related. A *W* is simply a double *V*. Both letters are composed of backward-slanting and forward-slanting lines.

Give the children some practice in making the backward-slanting and forward-slanting lines on the blackboard. Have them draw back and forth over the same line several times for each of these strokes.

After the children have practiced these lines, they should use them to make the two letters of today's lesson. Help them to see that small *v* compares with small *w* just the same as capital *V* compares with capital *W*. They should also take special notice of the fact that the backward-slanting line has been "pulled" forward so much that it is *almost* straight up-and-down, but not quite. While this is a characteristic of all backward-slanting lines in slant print, it is particularly noticeable with these letters.

The children will especially need to watch their alignment with these two letters, so that the points of each stroke come just to the line and do not go above or below it.

*The children should trace the letters in rows one through four and copy each to the end of the row. The sentence in rows five and seven should be copied in rows six and eight. Row nine should be used to practice the letters *S* and *Z* in all four forms.

The stroke combinations of the letters *V* and *W* are as follows: *V* and *v*—b-s line, f-s line; *W* and *w*—b-s line, f-s line, b-s line, f-s line. (In *V* and *W* all the lines should be made from top to bottom.)

Lesson 28
Height, Spacing, and Alignment in Slant Print

Lesson 28 Height, Spacing, and Alignment in Slant Print

Jericho had a high wall.

59

Aim of the Lesson

To reinforce proper concepts of height, spacing, and alignment, and to teach the importance of these qualities in writing.

Instructions for the Teacher

Thoroughly review height, spacing, and alignment with the children. Look first at height and alignment. Explain to the children how these two areas are related. If every letter is exactly the right height, it will also be aligned with every other letter of the same height.

Refer to the letters *h* **and** *a* **of the word** *had* in the sentence at the top of the page. **Remind the children that all the letters of the alphabet in slant print are either one space high or two spaces high.** The letter *h* is two spaces high, while *a* is only half as high, or one space. Even if there would be no lines above the bottom line, *h* should still be twice as high as *a*.

Look at the word *Jericho* **to explain alignment.** The *e, r, i, c,* lower part of *h,* and *o* should all be even across the top. That means one should be able to draw a straight line across the tops of all these letters, touching each one. The dotted line gives something to go by in helping to make them even. **Each letter needs to be drawn right to the line so that it is even.** The tall letters need to be aligned to touch the top line, and all letters need to touch the bottom line at the right place. **Show the children examples of incorrect alignment and how it makes the writing look as compared with correctly aligned letters.**

Spacing demands somewhat more guesswork than height and alignment. Show the children the short and long dashes between the letters and words in the sample sentence. Explain that the dash represents the length of the space and that each dash between letters should be the same length. The long dashes between words should also be the same length. **If the children are not sure their letters are spaced** right, suggest that they draw in some light lines in a word or two to be sure.

*Have the children copy the sentence in the first line once on the second line, then give them the following work orally to write in the remainder of the spaces. "Take this red rope that you used to let us down, and put it in the window. Then all of your family shall stay in the house" (spell words if necessary). See if the children can guess who made that statement (the two spies sent to Jericho).

When the children are finished, evaluate the height, spacing, and alignment of their work. You may wish to check these areas in some of their other subjects also.

Practice Sentences

1. Rahab was kind to the spies.
2. Balaam did not obey willingly.
3. Joshua became the new leader.

Lesson 29

Finding Mistakes in Slant Print

Joshua asked God to let the

sun and the moon stand still,

so they could finish fighting.

God did what Joshua asked.

Answer Key

1—should be oval
2—down line missing
3—should be slanted
4—too close
5—poorly formed
6—not slanted
7—crossed too low
8—poorly formed
9—too close
10—too narrow
11—too high
12—too high
13—poorly formed
14—should be straight
15—poorly formed
16—too high
17—too short
18—too high

19—no dot
20—too low
21—too narrow
22—too wide
23—poorly formed
24—too wide

Aim of the Lesson

To teach the children to identify errors in writing as a means of helping them see errors in their own writing.

Instructions for the Teacher

Again in this lesson, as in Lesson 8, the children will be doing the evaluating. The mistakes which were put into the sentences in this lesson will likely be some of the same mistakes the children themselves are making. They should be able to see their own mistakes. **When the children have finished the lesson, have them tell you the mistakes that they sometimes make in their own writing.**

Before the children begin **this lesson, explain that it is very much like Lesson 8,** except that it is written in slant print instead of regular manuscript. There are spacing, height, alignment, slant, and letter formation errors in the lesson.

*Instruct the children to look carefully at each letter and word, and at the spaces between them, to be sure they find all the mistakes. They should draw short arrows pointing to each mistake. When they have finished finding the errors in all four lines, have them copy each sentence in the spaces immediately below. Each error should be corrected, without new errors made. In the last line they should practice the letters *V* and *W* (all four forms).

There are twenty-four errors in the two sentences.

Lesson 30
Reviewing Slant Print

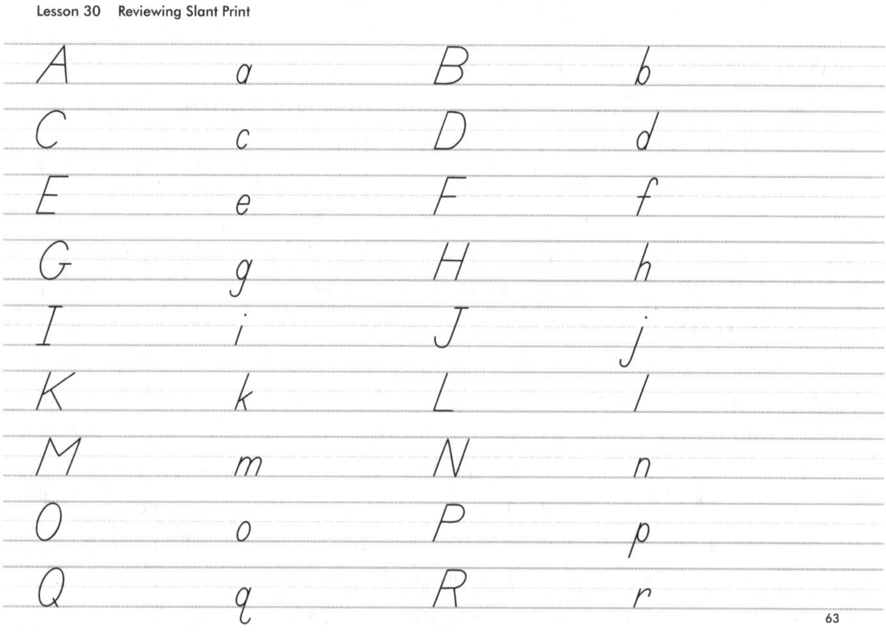

Lesson 30 Reviewing Slant Print

A a B b
C c D d
E e F f
G g H h
I i J j
K k L l
M m N n
O o P p
Q q R r

63

Aim of the Lesson

To review the slant letters thoroughly in preparation for the introduction of cursive writing.

Instructions for the Teacher

At the beginning of this class period, **go over the basic principles which make slant print different from regular manuscript writing.**

The two main principles are:

1. **Each stroke in slant print leans farther forward than the strokes of regular manuscript writing.**

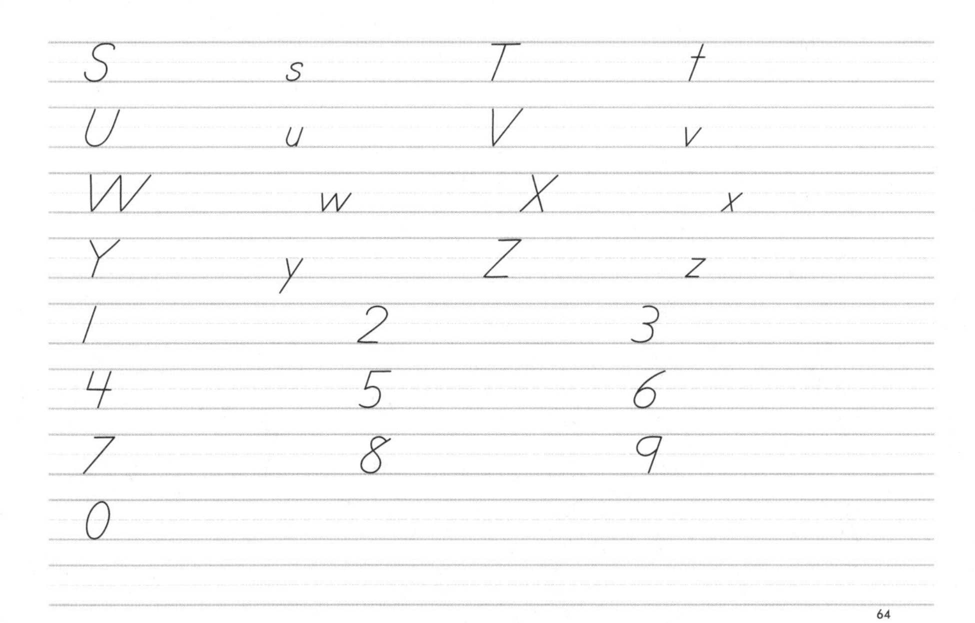

2. **The curves and circles of slant print are oval shaped rather than circle shaped.** An oval looks like a leaning, squashed circle. The oval has more of a pointed appearance than the circle.

At the blackboard the children should review the slant print strokes before doing the lesson.

*The children should copy each capital letter twice and each small letter three times in the space following. The numerals should each be copied three times.

Evaluate the children's work carefully to be sure they have caught the principles of slant print sufficiently well to prepare them for cursive writing. The important thing is to be sure they have the slant feel in their writing.

Practice Sentences

1. Achan sinned against God.
2. He was punished for his sin.
3. After that, God helped Israel.

Unit 2

Cursive Writing

Lessons 31–60

Stroke Formations of Cursive Letters

a—overcurve, oval, slant, undercurve
b—undercurve, slant, undercurve, retrace, undercurve
c—overcurve, overcurve, undercurve
d—overcurve, oval, slant, retrace, undercurve
e—undercurve, slant, undercurve
f—undercurve, slant, undercurve, undercurve
g—overcurve, oval, slant, overcurve
h—undercurve, slant, overcurve, slant, undercurve
i—undercurve, slant, undercurve, dot
j—undercurve, slant, overcurve, dot
k—undercurve, slant, overcurve, undercurve, slant, undercurve
l—undercurve, slant, undercurve
m—overcurve, slant, overcurve, slant, overcurve, slant, undercurve
n—overcurve, slant, overcurve, slant, undercurve
o—overcurve, oval undercurve
p—undercurve, slant, retrace, oval, undercurve
q—overcurve, oval, slant, undercurve, undercurve
r—undercurve, undercurve, slant, undercurve
s—undercurve, undercurve, undercurve
t—undercurve, slant, undercurve, across line
u—undercurve, slant, undercurve, slant, undercurve
v—overcurve, slant, undercurve, retrace, undercurve
w—undercurve, slant, undercurve, slant, undercurve, retrace, undercurve
x—overcurve, slant, undercurve, forward-slanting line
y—overcurve, slant, undercurve, slant, overcurve
z—overcurve, slant, hook, undercurve, overcurve

A—oval, slant, undercurve
B—undercurve, slant, overcurve, undercurve, overcurve, undercurve, undercurve
C—loop, overcurve, undercurve
D—double curve, double curve, overcurve, undercurve
E—loop, overcurve, undercurve, overcurve, undercurve
F—loop, double curve, double curve, undercurve, slant
G—undercurve, undercurve, undercurve, undercurve
H—loop, slant, overcurve, slant, overcurve, undercurve
I—overcurve, undercurve, undercurve
J—overcurve, slant, overcurve
K—loop, slant, double curve, overcurve, slant, under-curve
L—undercurve, slant, undercurve, double curve
M—loop, slant, overcurve, slant, overcurve, slant, undercurve
N—loop, slant, overcurve, slant, undercurve
O—large oval, undercurve
P—undercurve, slant, overcurve, undercurve
Q—loop, undercurve, double curve
R—undercurve, slant, overcurve, undercurve, overcurve, slant, undercurve
S—undercurve, double curve, undercurve
T—loop, double curve, double curve, undercurve
U—loop, slant, undercurve, slant, undercurve
V—loop, slant, double curve
W—loop, undercurve, undercurve, slant, overcurve
X—loop, undercurve, overcurve, undercurve
Y—loop, slant, undercurve, slant, overcurve
Z—loop, undercurve, undercurve, overcurve

Lesson 31
Introducing Cursive Writing

Lesson 31 Introducing Cursive Writing

God could not help
His people in battle
until they got rid of
the sin among them.
The people killed Achan
with stones.

67

Aim of the Lesson

To introduce the children to cursive writing; to help them understand the difference between cursive and manuscript writing.

Instructions for the Teacher

This lesson is simply an introduction to cursive writing. Do not expect the children to write cursive until they have learned the composition of the letters they are writing in terms of strokes.

There are a number of things you will want to mention as you look at this lesson with the children. First of all, **have the children look**

with you at the writing in the first four lines of the lesson. Explain that this kind of writing is called cursive writing. Have the children compare cursive writing with manuscript writing (slant print is a form of manuscript writing) by discussing the differences between the two. They should notice that all the letters within a word are joined. They should also notice that some cursive letters are not at all similar to their manuscript counterparts. Have them look for letters that they do not recognize, and discuss them briefly.

You should also mention the fact that all the cursive letters are made up of strokes, just as manuscript letters are. But cursive and manuscript letters are not made with all the same strokes. In later lessons they will learn what some of the different strokes are and how to form them.

*The children should copy the sentence printed in slant print two times in the space following.

Lesson 32
Recognizing Cursive Letters

Lesson 32 Recognizing Cursive Letters

z q f g y j
p d t b k h
l e r s o a
x v m n c w
u i X Z Q W
Y U V M N K
H I J R B P
T F D L G S
E C A O

69

Aim of the Lesson

To teach the association of cursive letters with their slant print and manuscript counterparts.

Instructions for the Teacher

***Following each cursive letter in this lesson, the children should print the slant print letter that corresponds with it. They will probably need to look at the alphabets in the back of the book for help** in identifying some letters. In fact, you should encourage them to do so if they have any questions at all, since the whole point of this lesson is learning to identify the cursive letters by name and association.

After the children have finished the lesson, ask them for their question about any particular letter which they may wonder about. **Discuss some of the more odd-shaped letters,** such as capital *T,* capital *F,* and capital *G.* If the children express doubt that they will ever be able to write some of these letters, explain that when they learn the strokes that make up these letters, these letters will not be so difficult as they look.

The children should not be careless with the formation of their slant print letters, even though the main emphasis is on learning the cursive letters. So be sure the children are making the slant print letters properly.

Practice Sentences

1. Israel served Moab 18 years.
2. Ehud helped to deliver them.
3. God used a nail to help Israel.

Lesson 33
Learning to Make Cursive Ovals

Lesson 33 Learning to Make Cursive Ovals

Gideon feared the angel.

Gideon feared the angel.

71

Aim of the Lesson

To help the children get the feel of cursive oval movement by teaching them to make sets of multiple ovals.

Instructions for the Teacher

Begin today's lesson by **looking at the examples of ovals and multiple ovals on the first two lines** of the lesson. Explain to the children that in this lesson they will learn how to make sets of these multiple ovals.

First of all, **demonstrate the multiple oval,** then **have the**

children draw the oval movements in the air at their seats along with you. This will help them to get the feel of the oval movement. Next **they should go to the blackboard for practice.** They should first **practice a few large single ovals, then several sets of large multiple ovals** with about ten ovals each.

Try to help the children make their ovals neatly. Each oval should be very close to the one right before it. The tops should be as nearly the same height as possible. You should practice the multiple oval yourself ahead of time so that you can demonstrate it neatly.

*In the lesson itself, the children should fill the spaces with sets of multiple ovals about the same length as those given in the lesson. (The multiple oval procedure is shown in three steps.) Every other row should be filled with small ovals. In the last three rows, the children should compare the cursive and slant print writing of the sentence, then copy it in slant print.

The children should try to make the large ovals with arm movement, if possible. However, if not possible, **they should use finger movement to make the up-and-down movement and work across the page with arm movement.** Likely very few will be able to learn to make the small oval movements with the whole arm.

Be satisfied that your children have mastered this technique at least to some degree before moving on.

Lesson 34
Learning to Make Cursive "Ups and Downs"

Lesson 34 Learning to Make Cursive "Ups and Downs"

Gideon was bold for God.

Gideon was bold for God.

73

Aim of the Lesson

To help the children get the feel of cursive up-and-down movement by teaching them to make sets of multiple slant lines.

Instructions for the Teacher

Send the children to the blackboard at the beginning of this class period to **review the multiple ovals.** They should make several sets of ten ovals each.

Demonstrate to the children how they should make the "ups

and downs." They should begin each set of "ups and downs" with a slightly undercurved up line, then make ten sets of up-and-down lines, ending with a slightly overcurved up line.

Have the children practice the "ups and downs" in the air and on the blackboard until they get the feel of the exercise. Be sure they are making these forms neatly. **Each line should have the same slant as all the other slants; each line should be equally spaced from each other line; and each line should be touching the top and bottom lines.**

Have the children practice this exercise until you are satisfied with their work, then **have them proceed with the lesson** according to the directions.

*In the first six rows, the children should alternate rows of full height "ups and downs" with half-height "ups and downs." In rows seven through nine, they should again compare the cursive with the slant print writing, then copy the sentence "Gideon was bold for God" on the final line in slant print.

Check your left-handers. Are they slanting their papers correctly? Are they **pushing** (not pulling) their downstrokes?

Practice Sentences

1. Gideon divided his men into three groups.
2. Each man had a trumpet and a pitcher.
3. The Midianites were afraid of Gideon.

Lesson 35
Cursive Ovals

Lesson 35 Cursive Ovals

O O O o o o O A o a

Jephthah kept the

promise he made

to God.

75

Aim of the Lesson

To teach the children the cursive oval stroke and its place in letters made with ovals.

Instructions for the Teacher

Begin the lesson by having the children draw "ups and downs" and multiple ovals a number of times on the blackboard. **Next they should draw a number of single ovals.** Have them do this in the air first, then on the blackboard, the same style as for slant print. Explain to the children that the cursive oval is a part of both cursive writing and slant print.

Insist that the children make both their multiple and single ovals evenly and with a free-flowing movement. This cannot be overemphasized. In slant print there is not so much emphasis on movement as there is in cursive. From now on it will be considered an important part of penmanship. **The movement should be whole-hand movement with as much arm movement as possible, not just finger movement.** If the children are sitting there **drawing** their ovals in a meticulous, finger-cramping manner, drilling on the oval stroke is of little value. **It is imperative that the children get the feel of the oval movement.**

Have the children go back to their seats and look at the first line of the lesson. **Show them how ovals are used in the small and capital letters** *O* **and** *A*. Do not have them write the letters at this point, but simply show them how the oval stroke is used in making the letters. This will help them to see that, in order to write these letters well, they will need to learn to make the oval stroke well.

*Have the children fill row two with multiple ovals, and row three with individual ovals (half of them large and half small). In rows five, seven, and nine, the children are to copy the sentence from the lines above, in slant print.

Note that beginning with this lesson the cursive writing is no longer "translated" to slant print for the children. This means that they will have to write without a direct standard to pattern after and that they will have to know the cursive letters. Do not let them become careless in their writing because of this; and if they have trouble recognizing any letters, have them find those letters in the alphabet at the back of the book.

Lesson 36
Cursive Slant Strokes

Lesson 36 Cursive Slant Strokes

l i t P a

Samson used fire and

foxes to burn the

crops.

77

Aim of the Lesson

To teach the children the cursive slant stroke and its place in letters made with slant lines.

Instructions for the Teacher

Begin the lesson by **having the children again review the multiple ovals and "ups and downs" on the blackboard.** Then **have them draw a number of individual slant lines in the air, then on the blackboard.** Explain to them that these slant lines that are used in cursive writing fill an important place in many cursive letters. It is important to learn them well.

Call the children's attention to the five capital and small letters in the first line and **have them identify the slant lines in each.**

Endeavor to have the children get the feel of the movement of making slant lines. Remind them that these slant lines that they will use in cursive writing are the same slant as the down lines of slant print. They are not the same as regular manuscript slant lines.

Explain also that some of the slant lines will be short and some of them will be tall. Some will even cover more than two lines in height. Call their attention to the letter *f* in the word *foxes* (in the practice sentence) to illustrate this.

*The children should fill row two with "ups and downs," and they should fill row three with single slant lines (half of them large and half small). The fifth, seventh, and ninth rows should be used to copy the cursive sentence from the lines above in slant print.

Remember, lots of practice on both the oval and the slant line is important. Practice forms the basis for future good writing habits.

Practice Sentences

1. Samson was a strong man.
2. He carried away the city gate.
3. He broke the ropes that held him.

Lesson 37
Cursive Undercurve Strokes

Lesson 37 Cursive Undercurve Strokes

r t i w h N L B

Samson killed many

people when he died.

79

Aim of the Lesson

To teach the children the cursive undercurve stroke and its place in letters made with undercurves.

Instructions for the Teacher

Demonstrate on the blackboard **how the undercurve stroke is taken from the oval.** Show that it is part of an oval. **Draw a number of undercurve strokes on the board, then have the children draw the stroke a number of times in the air.**

Have the children come to the blackboard and practice the

undercurve stroke for several minutes under your supervision. First have them go back and forth on the same undercurve several times as you count. At count one they should make the undercurve up; at count two, make it down, and so forth. Then have them raise their chalk for the down motion, making just the bottom-to-top curve. The strokes should be separated and made in rows across the blackboard. Have the children practice the strokes long enough that they get the feel of making them.

Explain to the children that some undercurves look as though they were lying down. Show how the undercurve is made in the ending strokes of some letters like the letter *t*. Explain also that some undercurves are made from the large oval, and some from the small oval. Those that come from the small oval only come to the middle line.

Have the children identify the undercurve strokes in the letters in row four before they proceed with the lesson.

*In rows two and three, the children should practice the short and long undercurve to the end of the row. In rows six and eight, they should copy the cursive sentence in slant print. In row nine, they should practice several sets of both the large and small multiple ovals.

Check your children's posture as they do this lesson. Be sure they are sitting up straight with both feet on the floor. Their papers should be positioned correctly, and pencils held properly. Also check your left-handers again for these things.

Lesson 38
Cursive Overcurve Strokes

Lesson 38 Cursive Overcurve Strokes

m q z J d y o C I

Ruth chose to serve

the true God.

81

Aim of the Lesson

To teach the children the cursive overcurve stroke and its place in letters made with overcurves.

Instructions for the Teacher

Go to the blackboard and **demonstrate the overcurve stroke. Show that it, as well as the under curve stroke, is taken from the oval.**

Have the children practice the overcurve in the air, then on the blackboard. Repeat a drill similar to that used in the

last lesson. As you count, they should draw back and forth on the overcurve (one up, two down, and so forth) several times. Next have them practice just the up overcurve, drawing on count one and raising the chalk for count two. For this second exercise, the strokes should be separated.

The children should practice these strokes long enough to get the feel of making them. While at the board they should review the undercurve stroke also.

Have the children identify the overcurves in the letters in row four. As with undercurves, overcurves sometimes lie down more than the demonstration strokes do in row one. The letters *g, z,* and *d* are examples of that. Sometimes, also, the overcurve may take a steeper curve than shown in the demonstration strokes. The capital letter *I* is an example of this.

*In rows two and three, the children should practice the short and long overcurves to the end of the row. In rows six and eight, they should copy the cursive sentence in slant print. In row nine, have them practice several sets of both the multiple ovals and the "ups and downs."

Practice Sentences

1. Ruth was willing to work.
2. She went out into the fields.
3. Ruth helped Naomi make a living.

Lesson 39
Cursive Loop Strokes

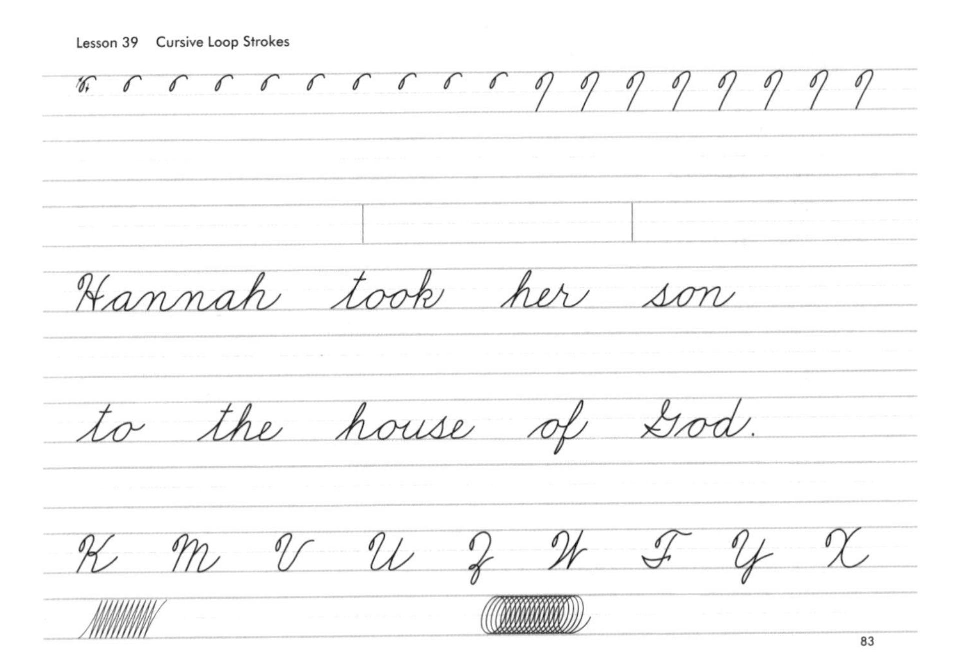

Aim of the Lesson

To teach the children the cursive loop stroke and its place in letters made with cursive loops.

Instructions for the Teacher

Have the children draw the "ups and downs' and multiple ovals in the air as a warmup for this lesson.

Demonstrate the formation of the loop stroke on the blackboard. Explain that this loop stroke is used only in capital letters, and not even in all of them; but it is important to learn it. The letters in row eight are some of the letters that use loops.

Explain that the loop stroke is actually a combination of two strokes, a short undercurve stroke, then a larger overcurve. The undercurve starts almost at the top line, then slants down and slightly backward to the middle line. Here the overcurve begins and goes back up toward the top line, touching the top of the undercurve on its way. When it reaches the top line, it curves down again. Looking at the letters in row eight, show the children how the loop stroke is connected to the first down line of each capital letter (except *Z, F,* and *X*). **On the blackboard draw the loop stroke several times connected with the first down line as shown in the last part of row one.**

Have the children come to the blackboard and practice writing the loop stroke. After they have written the standard loop stroke, have them practice making the loop stroke along with the slant stroke, which is the way many letters are written.

*At their seats the children should proceed with the lesson. The strokes in row one should be copied directly below in row two. In row three, the children should review the oval, the undercurve, and the overcurve (large and small kinds). The sentence in rows four and six should be copied in slant print in rows five and seven. The last row is for practice of the "ups and downs" and multiple ovals.

Lesson 40
Cursive Retrace Strokes

Lesson 40 Cursive Retrace Strokes

b v w b v w

Eli died when the

ark was taken.

85

Aim of the Lesson

To teach the children the cursive retrace stroke and its place in letters made with retraces.

Instructions for the Teacher

Have the children practice the multiple ovals and "ups and downs" in the air as a warmup exercise.

Introduce the retrace stroke and draw it on the blackboard. Explain that the word *retrace* means "to go back over." The top part of the undercurve is the part to be retraced. Show the children the retrace combination, which is an undercurve, **retrace,** then another undercurve. Explain that the retrace is most often used in three letters—*b, v,* and *w.*

At the blackboard the children should practice the combination given in row one. Watch them closely, and be sure they keep an even motion, maintaining the feel of the undercurve stroke. Since this is the first time they are combining three strokes, **they must learn to make a smooth transition from the undercurve to the retrace stroke and from the retrace to the final undercurve.** They should practice this over and over again until they can do it smoothly, accurately, and neatly.

When teaching **the retrace stroke, be sure the children are not making it too long or too short.** If the retrace is too long, it tends to make the letter difficult to identify. If the retrace is too short or nonexistent, a level across (or curve) line will be substituted for the undercurve.

The children should identify the retrace strokes in the letters in row four prior to doing the lesson.

*The stroke combinations in row one should be copied in rows two and three. The sentence in rows five and seven should be copied in slant print in rows six and eight. In row nine, the oval, overcurve, undercurve, and slant line should be practiced in the spaces following those strokes.

Practice Sentences

1. Dagon was an idol.
2. God punished those who took the ark.
3. The ark did not belong to them.

Lesson 41
Joining Undercurves and Slants

Lesson 41 Joining Undercurves and Slants

Saul became the king.

87

Aim of the Lesson

To teach the children how to make the undercurve and slant strokes together.

Instructions for the Teacher

Explain to the children that now they have learned to make all the individual strokes of the cursive style of writing. But **letters** are not made of individual strokes alone; they are rather made of **combinations of strokes.**

The children have already learned the retrace stroke combination made up of an undercurve, retrace, and undercurve. **The combination they will learn now is the undercurve-slant combination.** Actually there are two different combinations looked at in this lesson, one with one undercurve and one slant, and the other with an additional undercurve at the end.

On the blackboard explain and demonstrate the undercurve-slanting combination as shown at the beginning of row one. Make several of them to show the children what motions are used in making them. **Have them make several of these combinations** in the air as you count one for the undercurve and two for the slant. Next **have them make the three-stroke combination the same way** as you count.

The children should practice the stroke combinations at the blackboard. Be sure they practice each combination enough to be able to form them effortlessly, automatically, and accurately.

*In row one, the children should trace each stroke combination given. In rows two and three, they should trace each set of stroke combinations and make several of each in the space following. Rows four and five should be filled with the stroke combination given at the beginning of row four, and rows six and seven should be filled with the stroke combination given at the beginning of row six. The sentence in row eight should be copied in row nine in slant print.

Lesson 42
Joining Overcurves and Slants

Lesson 42 Joining Overcurves and Slants

Saul gave God praise.

89

Aim of the Lesson

To teach the children how to make the overcurve and slant strokes together.

Instructions for the Teacher

Have the children come to the blackboard and **review the undercurve-slant combination.**

After the children are seated, **demonstrate how to make the overcurve-slant combination. Emphasize the connecting point between the two strokes.** As you draw the combination a number of times, show the importance of making it smoothly rounded (/\ ), not sharply pointed (/|).

Have the children practice the overcurve-slant combination in the air, then have them come to the blackboard and practice making it as you count for each stroke. Have them practice until you are confident they can do it rhythmically, smoothly, and accurately.

*In row one, the children should fill each space with the type of stroke combination that immediately precedes it. In rows two and three, the children should make several sets of multiple combinations. In rows four and five, they should copy the stroke at the beginning of row four. Follow the same procedure in rows six and seven. The sentence in row eight should be copied in row nine in slant print.

Practice Sentences

1. The people sacrificed to the Lord.
2. God sent thunder and rain.
3. Samuel told Saul he had sinned.

Lesson 43
Making Loops in Small Letters

Lesson 43 Making Loops in Small Letters

91

Aim of the Lesson

To teach the children to form neat upper and lower loops.

Instructions for the Teacher

Demonstrate on the blackboard the formation of all four types of small letter loops shown in this lesson. **With the first two types, compare each with its counterpart which does not have a loop,** the *t* and *i* combinations. Show that with each, the two forms are made the same way except that, to make the loop combination, one must **put a little hook on the end of the undercurve**

before coming down with the slant. **The hook creates the loop effect.** (Note that this is not called a loop stroke as in Lesson 39.)

The third form is made of a slant line and an overcurve line. Again a slight hook should be made, this time on the end of the slant line before making the overcurve. **In the fourth form, the slant line is made the same as in the third form, but the curve is an undercurve stroke.** It goes in the opposite direction and comes back to the slant at the bottom line.

With each of these loop combinations, it is important to **help the children learn to make the connecting point properly. The slant line and the curve line should both be distinct.** The connecting point should be neither extremely pointed nor so rounded that one cannot discern where it is.

In these combinations you should **insist that the children make the loops wide enough to be easily seen.** Teaching them to make a well-formed loop from the very beginning will eliminate some problems in future years.

Have the children come to the blackboard and practice each of these strokes until they become efficient in making them accurately and effortlessly.

*In the first eight rows, the stroke combination in each odd row should be copied in that row, then in the following even row. The children should copy each stroke combination in row nine at least once in the space immediately following.

Be sure your children are maintaining **good posture,** both at the blackboard and at their seats.

Lesson 44
Making Cursive Letters From Strokes (Part 1)

Lesson 44 Making Cursive Letters From Strokes (Part 1)

o

David became king next.

93

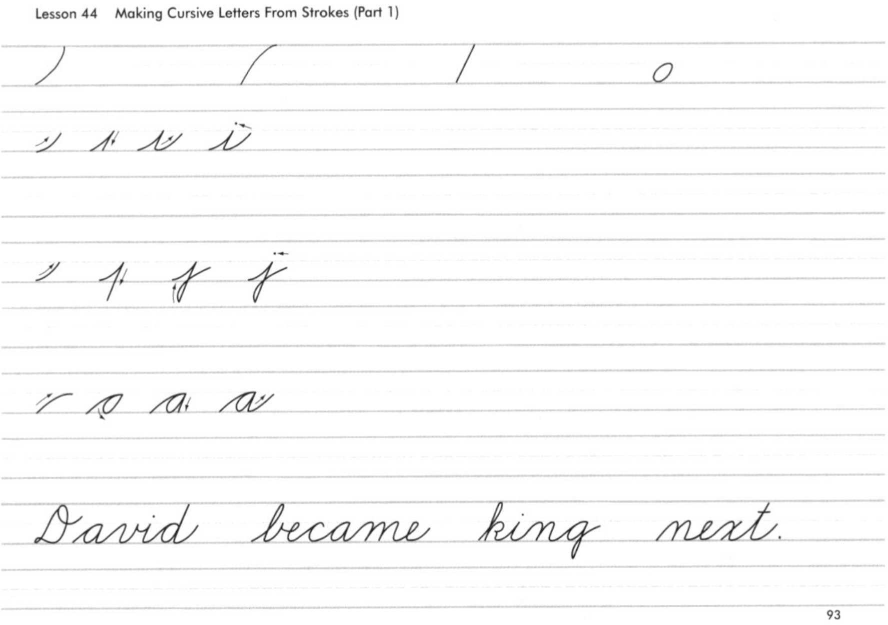

Aim of the Lesson

To teach the children how letters are made up of different combinations of strokes.

Instructions for the Teacher

Place the letters *t, y,* **and** *o* **on the blackboard. Have the children identify** the strokes in each one.

Next **demonstrate how these strokes are put together correctly into letters.** Draw each letter stroke by stroke, showing how the entire letter is made by smoothly drawing all the strokes together. Write each one several times, showing the children the feel and movement of making cursive letters.

Have the children practice some of the basic strokes, then form the letters you have demonstrated. **They should make each letter twice, then make several more as you count strokes.** Be sure they get the feel of each letter well, then have them also work on the letters *i, j,* and *a,* the letters in the lesson.

*In row one, the children should practice each stroke in the space following. They should copy the letter *i* in rows two and three, the letter *j* in rows four and five, and the letter *a* in rows six and seven. The sentence in row eight should be copied in slant print in row nine.

As the children work their lesson, be sure they have **good posture** and are **holding their pencils correctly.** Check their letter making to be sure they are forming them both smoothly and accurately. Both areas are important. As you watch their movement, you should be able to discern whether they have the feel of each letter.

Practice Sentences

1. Saul sinned more by telling a lie.
2. God does not see as men see.
3. David had God's Spirit in him.

Lesson 45
Making Cursive Letters From Strokes (Part 2)

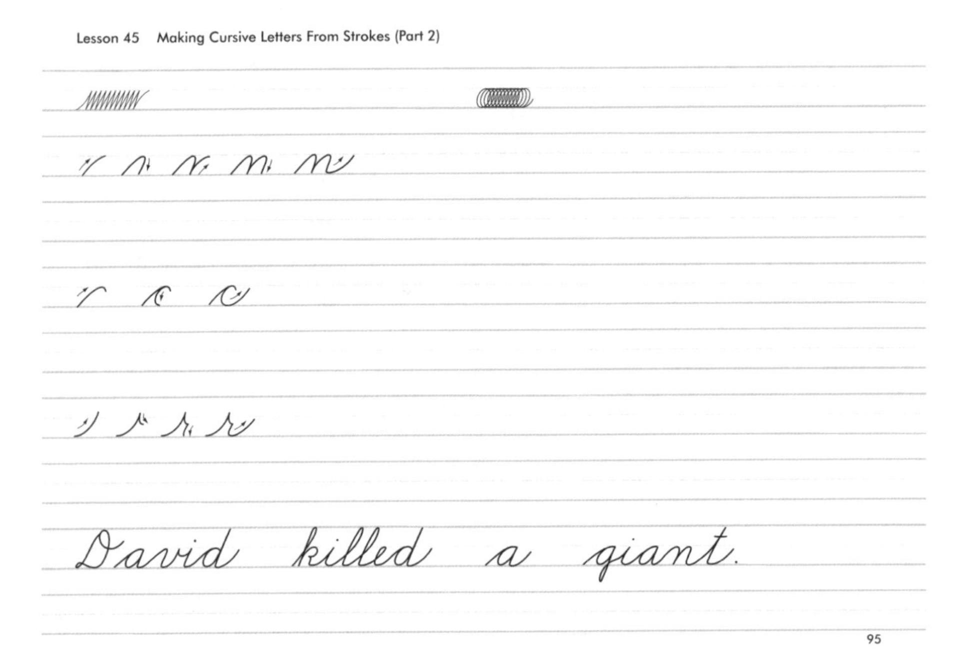
Lesson 45 Making Cursive Letters From Strokes (Part 2)

David killed a giant.

95

Aim of the Lesson

To teach the children how letters are made up of different combinations of strokes.

Instructions for the Teacher

Write the letters *m, l,* **and** *u* **on the blackboard. Ask the children some questions about these letters,** such as: Which of these letters begin(s) with an undercurve? an overcurve? Which letter has three overcurves? Which forms a loop? Which has three slant lines? three undercurves?

Have the children come to the blackboard and practice making multiple "ups and downs" and multiple ovals, then have them practice *m, l,* **and** *u.* Be on hand to help them in forming the letters. They should make each letter stroke by stroke. Help them to make each stroke join with each other stroke correctly. Then have them practice these letters while you count strokes for them.

Send the children back to their seats. With their books open, **demonstrate and explain the letters** *n, c,* **and** *r.* **Have the children practice making these letters in the air, then on paper.**

*In row one, the children should make several sets of multiple "ups and downs" and ovals in the space following each figure. The letter *n* should be copied in rows two and three, the letter *c* in rows four and five, and the letter *r* in rows six and seven. The sentence in row eight should be copied in row nine in slant print.

One important thing to remember is that this lesson as well as the previous one simply teaches the children how to put strokes together to make letters. **Do not be very exacting at this point on details of correct formation,** since they will be going over all these letters more thoroughly later.

Lesson 46
Learning Cursive Overcurve Letters

Lesson 46 Learning Cursive Overcurve Letters

97

Aim of the Lesson

To teach the formation of the cursive overcurve letters.

Instructions for the Teacher

Have the children practice writing the overcurve in the air and on paper.

On the blackboard **demonstrate and explain each letter carefully to the children. Go over the strokes** that compose each letter, **and the important points mentioned below** in connection with each letter.

The letter *c* is made with an overcurve, an overcurve, and an undercurve. The second overcurve is made from the top to the bottom and is more sharply curved than the first one. The second overcurve and the undercurve should be joined with a quick, sharp curve near the bottom line.

The letter *m* is made with an overcurve, slant, overcurve, slant, overcurve, slant, and undercurve. The slant should be sharply distinguishable from the overcurve in each hump of the letter. Watch this closely, as it is a basic point to remember in making the letter.

The letter *n* is made with an overcurve, slant, overcurve, slant, and undercurve, making it identical with the letter *m* except that it has one less hump. Be sure the children realize that the cursive *m* and *n* both have one more hump than the manuscript *m* and *n*.

The letter *v* is made with an overcurve, slant, undercurve, retrace, and undercurve. Try to help the children make the slant and the undercurve join smoothly without a sharp point, yet not so rounded that the distinction between the slant line and the undercurve is not clear.

The letter *x* is made with an overcurve, a slant, and an undercurve and is crossed with a forward-slanting line. The forward-slanting line should be made from the top to the bottom, and it should cross the slant line exactly in the middle.

Following your explanation and demonstration, **the children should practice each letter on the blackboard briefly. They should memorize the stroke combinations** to the extent that they can recall them for each letter immediately upon being asked.

*The children should copy the letters in the space following each one.

You may wish to have the children copy the stroke layouts of the letters in the space immediately below each one before filling in the remaining space with practice letters.

Practice Sentences

1. David and Jonathan were friends.
2. The king did not like David.
3. Saul asked the priests to come to him.

Lesson 47
Learning Cursive Undercurve Letters

Lesson 47 Learning Cursive Undercurve Letters

99

Aim of the Lesson

To teach the formation of the cursive undercurve letters.

Instructions for the Teacher

Have the children practice writing the undercurve in the air and on paper.

Demonstrate and explain each letter carefully to the children. **Go over the strokes that compose each letter, and the important points mentioned below in connection with each letter.**

The letter *i* is made with an undercurve, slant, undercurve, and a dot. The children should practice this letter extensively to get the feel of making it well, as it is a basic stroke pattern. It is a good letter for counting strokes. Say, "One, two, three, dot; one, two, three, dot; one, two . . ." The bottom of the slant line should make a fairly distinct point where it joins the final undercurve.

The letter *u* is made with an undercurve, slant, undercurve, slant, and undercurve. The basic pattern is the same as that of the letter *i*. The children should be careful to make all of their undercurve-slant combinations the same so that each letter looks balanced.

The letter *w* is made with an undercurve, slant, undercurve, slant, undercurve, retrace, and undercurve. Each of the three stems of this letter should be exactly the same distance apart, with undercurves and slants made the same each time (except for the final undercurve). Be sure the retrace comes down nearly halfway, neither all the way to the bottom line as a full slant, nor so short as to be virtually nonexistent.

The letter *r* is made with an undercurve, undercurve, slant, and undercurve. This letter does not follow a basic combination pattern. The first undercurve is made normally except that it goes a short distance above the middle line. The second undercurve is very short and is made the opposite way from the first undercurve, coming down one-third space from the middle line. From the end of the second undercurve, a short slant is made to the bottom line; then the final undercurve is drawn at the end. **Give the children plenty of practice in making and joining the first two undercurves so as to produce a well-formed letter.**

The letter *s* is made of three undercurves, all different. The first undercurve is made like the first one in the letter *r*. It goes up just beyond the middle line. The second undercurve starts out almost like a slant line but then it starts curving back near the bottom, touches the bottom line, then meets the first undercurve at a point just above the bottom line. The third undercurve goes forward along the second undercurve line for a short distance, then goes on out to form the ending stroke of the letter.

Have the children practice the letters from Lesson 46 first, then have them work on the letters from this lesson on the blackboard. Again **they should memorize the stroke combinations.**

*The children should copy the letters in the space following each one. The letters again are arranged so that the children can first copy the stroke layout of each letter on the lines immediately below if you so desire.

Lesson 48
Learning Cursive Lower-loop Letters

Lesson 48 Learning Cursive Lower-loop Letters

101

Aim of the Lesson

To teach the formation of the cursive lower-loop letters.

Instructions for the Teacher

Before looking at the individual lower-loop letters with the children, **go over some helps related to the basic characteristics of these letters.**

Explain and demonstrate how the lower-loop part of each

letter is made with a slant line and an overcurve. In the letter *z*, however, the lower loop is more rounded.

With all the below-the-line letters, **the children will have to learn how far down to bring the slant line.** It should go down one space, but they will also have to estimate the distance.

The children will need to **pay attention to the point of junction between the slant line and the overcurve at the bottom of the loop.** The joining point should be sharp enough that a definite distinction can be seen between the two strokes.

Do not let the children curve the slant line or make the overcurve too large. Either of these will result in **a loop that is too rounded and wide.**

Also explain to the children that **the final stroke should cross** the previous one in each of these letters **exactly at the bottom line,** not above or below it.

Demonstrate and explain the letters below **by going over the strokes that compose each letter** on the blackboard and by **discussing the important points mentioned in connection with each letter.**

The letter *j* is made with an undercurve, slant, overcurve, and dot. Be sure the children do not forget the dot.

The letter *g* is made with an overcurve, oval, slant, and overcurve. Help your pupils form the oval neatly. Be sure they have acquired the feel of the oval.

The letter *y* is made with an overcurve, slant, undercurve, slant, and overcurve. They should have little difficulty with this letter.

The letter *z* is made with an overcurve, slant, hook, undercurve, and overcurve. If the children make all the strokes in this letter carefully, it should be fairly accurate. One thing you will need to watch is that the hook does not get too big. It should be made very small and sharp. Also you should give the children special help with the joining of the undercurve and the final overcurve. They should make a long, narrow loop, not a large, wide one.

*Have the children copy the letters in the space following each stroke layout. (They may first practice the layouts of each letter in the space immediately below.) In the last row, they should copy the slant strokes in the space following each one.

Although you are concentrating on the formation of these letters and not primarily on the quality of writing, you should be sure that the children's alignment and slant are not too far off.

Practice Sentences

1. Saul took three thousand men to search.
2. Saul changed his mind often.
3. David trusted in God to help him.

Lesson 49
Learning Cursive Upper-loop Letters

Lesson 49 Learning Cursive Upper-loop Letters

103

Aim of the Lesson

To teach the formation of the cursive upper-loop letters.

Instructions for the Teacher

Draw a simple upper-loop form composed of an undercurve and a slant **on the blackboard as a reference point** to use for further explanation. The children should remember learning this combination earlier. **Give the children the guidelines in the following**

paragraphs for this kind of letter. Some of these principles have been given previously, but you will need to reteach them in this lesson for the children's benefit.

Help the children put the correct amount of curve into the undercurve that begins each of these letters. The degree of curve in the first undercurve affects the size of the loop and where the slant line and undercurve cross.

The children should be careful to make the hook at the top end of the undercurve neither too rounded and wide nor too small. The hook also affects the size and the shape of the loop, **which must be moderately narrow, but noticeable.**

The slant line must be straight. Curving the slant line is a lazy way of writing. Insist on straight slant lines in all letters with upper loops, and you will have helped your pupils learn a very important lesson in neat handwriting.

Go over the strokes of each upper-loop letter with the children, discussing any **important points** mentioned in connection with any of the letters.

The letter *f* is made with an undercurve, slant, undercurve, and undercurve. This letter is one of the tallest letters; therefore, the children may have a problem making the slant line straight over such a long distance.

The letter *e* is made with an undercurve, a slant line, and an undercurve. This is the only short upper-loop letter. Due to its shortness, it may be difficult to get the slant line as distinct as it should be. Have the children form this letter carefully and accurately, stroke by stroke, and pick up speed gradually. As they continue working with this letter in the future, you will have to **make sure this letter maintains a straight back side** and does not degenerate into the big, round circle that it so often becomes. The other extreme is making the loop too small or even nonexistent.

The letter *l* is made with an undercurve, slant, and undercurve. It is basically the same as the letter *e,* except it is two spaces high. Watch the size of the loop on this letter.

The letter *b* is made with an undercurve, slant, undercurve, retrace, and undercurve. With this letter you may need to counter the tendency of some children to make the bottom of the letter horseshoe shaped (*b*). A good slant line-undercurve combination will not look like a horseshoe at the bottom. They should also learn to make the retrace part of the letter neatly.

The letter *k* is made with an undercurve, slant, overcurve, undercurve, slant, and undercurve. The first part of this letter is like the letter *l*. It will take some practice for the children to fully master the last part. The overcurve in the last part of the letter goes to the middle line. The next stroke, an undercurve, curves backward to a point not quite touching the overcurve and about halfway between the middle and bottom lines. From that point, one draws a very short slant line to the bottom line before finishing with a final undercurve.

The letter *h* is made with an undercurve, slant, overcurve, slant, and undercurve. It is basically like the letter *k,* except it does not have the backward undercurve following the overcurve.

The children should practice each of the letters on the blackboard. Be sure they understand the principles behind the formation of each letter.

*Have the children copy each letter in the space following. They may copy the stroke layouts in the space directly below each one.

Lesson 50
Learning Cursive Oval Letters

Aim of the Lesson

To teach the formation of the cursive oval letters.

Instructions for the Teacher

To introduce the lesson, have the children look at the three letters in this lesson and **pick out the ovals in each letter.** Have them look back over the alphabet for three other letters that contain an oval. They are the letters *p, d,* and *g.* The reason *g* is not included in this lesson is that the children have already learned to make it in Lesson 48. And both *p* and *d* will be taught in the next lesson.

Demonstrate each letter individually, discussing the stroke formation of each one **and the important points mentioned** in connection with them.

The letter *a* is made with an overcurve, oval, slant, and undercurve. Since the letter *a* is one of the most commonly used letters of the alphabet, it is quite necessary that the children learn it right. One important item that is frequently neglected is closing the oval. **You must insist that they close every oval** carefully at the top. **It is also important that there be a proper relationship between the oval and the slant.** The slant should not follow the side of the oval the entire distance to the bottom line. Rather, it should separate from the oval a short distance down from the top. Also, **the place where the slant and undercurve join should not be rounded, but should make a distinct point.**

The letter *o* is made with an overcurve, an oval, and an undercurve. With this letter again, you will need to watch that they close the oval properly. **Also watch the final undercurve.** Some children go to extremes in making this curve, either drawing straight across (*o*) or bringing it down too far and making the letter look like a sloppily written *a* (*o*).

The letter *q* is made with an overcurve, oval, slant, undercurve, and undercurve. The children will quickly see the similarity between this letter and the letter *g*. The primary difference is that the loop in the letter *q* is backward from the loop in the letter *g*. It is made with an undercurve rather than an overcurve. With this letter again, you must watch that they close the oval properly. Also, the undercurve that forms the loop must meet the slant exactly at the bottom line.

The children should include the letter *g* as they practice these letters on the blackboard.

*Have the children copy the drills in row one in the space following each. The three letters should be copied in the space that follows them, and the stroke layouts should be copied on the line immediately below.

Practice Sentences

1. Jesus talked to His Father.
2. John warned people to be sorry for their sins.
3. Jesus preached to the people.

Lesson 51
Learning Cursive Letters With Tall Stems

Lesson 51 Learning Cursive Letters With Tall Stems

p p a

b

d d d

c

l t e

f g h i j k l

m n o q r s

u v w x y z

107

Aim of the Lesson

To teach the formation of the cursive letters with tall stems.

Instructions for the Teacher

Explain and demonstrate to the children the meaning of *stem* **in letters. The stem or stems in a letter are what make its sharp points.** In this lesson the children learn the tall-stem letters. They have already learned to make short-stem letters, such as *i, u,* and *w*. In addition to having a tall upper stem, the letter *p* has a lower stem that goes below the line, the only letter in the alphabet that does.

A stem is usually made with an undercurve and a slant. The letter *d* is a mild exception. There the undercurve part is made with a slant line connected to the final stroke of the oval and goes up to the top line.

Look at each letter individually with the children, going over the strokes and formation and discussing the important points mentioned in connection with each one.

The letter *p* is made with an undercurve, slant, retrace, oval, and undercurve. Have the children tell you what other letter they have learned that goes both up to the top line and down below the bottom line. (It is the letter *f*.) Be sure they make a solid stem, not a loop, in the bottom part of this letter.

The letter *d* is made with an overcurve, oval, slant, retrace, and undercurve. Show the children that the letter *d* is much like the letter *a,* except that the oval of the letter *d* has a tail that goes up to the top line. The slant line is also longer on the letter *d.* Here again they must be careful not to make a loop in the stem. They should also be sure they close the oval without leaving a gap.

The letter *t* is made with an undercurve, slant, undercurve, and across line borrowed from manuscript. This letter should cause no particular problems, since the basic undercurve-slant form has been already learned. Be sure the children make the meeting place of the slant and undercurve pointed, not rounded.

Have the children practice making these three letters on the blackboard as you supervise them. You may also wish to **have them practice the other letters of the alphabet once each.**

*The children should copy the stroke layouts of the three letters learned in this lesson in the space immediately below them. The space following the stroke layouts should be filled with practice letters. The space following each review letter of the alphabet is to be used to copy that letter one time.

As the children work this lesson, **give a quick check on their posture and pencil holding.** Are they slouching? pinching their pencils? leaning too far over their work?

Lesson 52
Joining Cursive Letters to Make Words (Part 1)

Lesson 52 Joining Cursive Letters to Make Words (Part 1)

father father father
father

mother mother
mother

children children
children

109

Aim of the Lesson

To teach the children how to join cursive letters properly in order to form words.

Instructions for the Teacher

The whole point of this lesson is learning to blend the final stroke of one letter with the beginning stroke of the next one. Call the children's attention to the different types of strokes which are blended between letters (as described in the next paragraphs).

Look with the children at the word *father.* First **discuss how the letters *f* and *a* in this word are joined.** The letter *f* ends with an undercurve and the letter *a* begins with an overcurve. How can these strokes be blended? Ask the children for their ideas, then explain and demonstrate. In joining the letters *f* and *a,* **the first half of the final undercurve of the letter *f* is combined with the last half of the beginning overcurve of the letter *a* to make the joining stroke. This principle applies every time two letters are joined.**

Also look with the children at the way in which the other letters of the word *father* are joined. They are all undercurve-to-undercurve blends; therefore, a simple undercurve from one letter to the next is made as a blending stroke.

In the word *mother,* a high, final undercurve from the letter *o* is blended with a regular undercurve from the beginning of the letter *t*. Show the children how this type of curve combination joins.

The children should practice joining letters by practice-writing these three words several times each on the blackboard. Be sure they are joining them correctly and smoothly. Especially help the children blend an undercurve with an overcurve neatly, as between the letters *f* and *a.*

*The children should fill in rows two and three with five copies of the word *father.* In rows four, five, and six, they should make six copies of the word *mother,* and in rows eight and nine, five copies of the word *children.* They should be careful to join all letters correctly.

Be sure the children are maintaining correct pencil-holding habits, as well as posture that contributes to neat writing.

Practice Sentences

1. Tell what great things the Lord has done.
2. We must hear God's Word and obey it.
3. A woman touched Jesus' clothes and was made well.

Lesson 53
Joining Cursive Letters to Make Words (Part 2)

Lesson 53 Joining Cursive Letters to Make Words (Part 2)

Jesus said that we

should go into all the

world and preach the

Gospel to everyone.

yes *give*

111

Aim of the Lesson

To teach the children how to join cursive letters neatly and correctly.

Instructions for the Teacher

In this lesson the children should learn how to join a final overcurve with a beginning overcurve, how to join a final overcurve with a beginning undercurve, and some guidelines for

joining capital letters to the words which they begin.

Look first with the children at **the joining of the** *g* **and** *o* **in** *go.* Explain as you demonstrate that **when two overcurves are blended in this manner, one large overcurve is all that is needed as a blending stroke.** Remind the children that the same principle applied with the joining of two undercurves. **Have them practice writing the word** *go* **in the air,** especially emphasizing the joining overcurve.

Next go to **the word** *yes,* looking at the blending of strokes in **the joining of the letters** *y* **and** *e.* **Here we have a final overcurve blended with a beginning undercurve.** When we blend these two strokes, **we get a double-curve effect.** The last part of the overcurve is dropped, along with the first part of the undercurve, and what is left is put together. Demonstrate as you explain, and **have the children practice the joining of the letters** *y* **and** *e* **in the air.**

Also in this lesson we have two capital letters, in the words *Jesus* and *Gospel.* The children should notice that one of the capital letters is not joined to the rest of the word. Explain that some capitals are joined to the word which they begin, and some are not. The rule is that **capital letters that end with a final undercurve** (such as *A, E,* and *R*) **or with an overcurve from a lower loop** (such as *J, Y,* and *Z*) **can be joined** to the words which they begin. **The capital letters** *B, D, F, G, H, I, L, O, P, Q, S, T, V,* **and** *W* **must not be joined** to the words they begin.

Be sure the children get sufficient practice in making the various types of letter joinings, then have them proceed with the lesson.

*The children should copy the sentence in rows one, three, five, and seven in the space immediately below. Watch them as they work to be sure they are blending strokes and joining letters neatly and accurately. Each word in row nine should be copied once in the space that follows.

Lesson 54
Learning Cursive Capitals With Undercurves

Lesson 54 Learning Cursive Capitals With Undercurves

113

Aim of the Lesson

To teach the children the basics of forming the six cursive capital letters beginning with undercurves.

Instructions for the Teacher

Explain to the children what the main differences are between capital cursive letters and small cursive letters. The main difference is that capital letters *always* go all the way to the top line, and small letters do not. Capital letters often have more strokes and look bigger than small letters. Capital letters are not quite as simple to make as small letters, for they have longer and more complicated strokes.

Tell the children that in this lesson they will be learning how to make the six capital letters that begin with undercurves, the letters *P, R, B, L, G,* and *S.* **Go over the strokes and formation of each letter with the children on the blackboard, as well as the important points mentioned in relation to each letter.**

The letter *P* is made with an undercurve, slant, overcurve, and undercurve. The first undercurve goes from the middle line to the top line. The slant goes from the top line to the bottom line, and the overcurve goes back up to the top line. The undercurve goes down to the middle line, then back up, stopping at the slant line.

The letter *R* is made with an undercurve, slant, overcurve, undercurve, overcurve, slant, and undercurve. The first part of the letter is made very much like the letter *P.* The last part is different. The undercurve that finishes out the top of the letter touches the slant just below the middle line, and the overcurve makes a small loop followed by a second slant to the bottom line. An undercurve finishes the letter. It is important, in this letter, that the second slant be straight, not curved. Also the overcurve-undercurve combination that forms the top should be made smoothly and carefully.

The letter *B* is made with an undercurve, slant, overcurve, undercurve, overcurve, undercurve, and undercurve. It is formed just like *R* down to the small loop at the middle line. From the end of this small loop, a large, full, and well-rounded undercurve should be made that goes around to the bottom line, then rises and meets the slant at a point above the bottom line. The children may not make this letter perfectly at first because of its many curves. Therefore, be patient and help them do the best they can.

The letter *L* is made with an undercurve, slant, undercurve, and double curve. The undercurve starts below the middle line, curves up gradually to the top line, then loops around, with a slant line going almost to the bottom line. An undercurve is made which touches the bottom line and loops back, with a double curve going below the bottom line to finish the letter. This letter also is mostly curves, so it may take some practice to get perfect.

The letter *G* is made with an undercurve, undercurve, undercurve, and undercurve. Yes, that is right: four undercurves.

However, they must be put together in a special way. The first undercurve curves gently from the bottom line to the top line. The second undercurve loops back and crosses the first undercurve just below the middle line, then comes up and touches the middle line. The third undercurve curves down, touches the bottom line, then crosses the first undercurve above the bottom line, and stops a short distance below the middle line. The fourth undercurve goes from that point and makes a short curve down and back across the first undercurve. Have the children remember that the first undercurve gets crossed by each of the other strokes in turn at some point in the letter.

The letter *S* is made with an undercurve, double curve, and final undercurve. It is made similarly to the letter *G* in some respects. It begins with the same kind of undercurve, which curves gently to the top line. Then the double curve loops in a figure-eight style to the bottom line and back up again, crossing the first undercurve just above the bottom line. From there the last undercurve crosses the first undercurve again, ending in the space between the first undercurve and the double curve.

No doubt **your second graders are going to have difficulty** with some of these capital letters. **The cursive capitals are being covered rapidly** and are somewhat complicated. Since capitals are used less frequently than small letters, **it is not necessary now to learn them thoroughly.** So do not let the children become discouraged. Explain that they shall do the best they can and next year they will learn them better. **If they cannot form a cursive capital well in sentence writing, they should be permitted at this point to use a slant print capital.**

*Have the children copy each stroke layout in the space immediately below it. Copies of the finished letters should be written in the remaining space following each letter.

Practice Sentences

(Beginning with this group, the children should write their practice sentences in cursive. They may change to cursive in their daily work at your discretion. As noted above, they may use slant print capitals until they master the cursive capitals.)

1. Jesus talked to His Father in heaven.
2. His disciples were rowing against the wind.
3. Jesus went to them on the water.

Lesson 55
Learning Cursive Capitals With Loops (Part 1)

Lesson 55 Learning Cursive Capitals With Loops

115

Aim of the Lesson

To teach the children to form neatly the cursive-loop capitals that begin with a loop and a slant line.

Instructions for the Teacher

The capital letters that begin with loops are divided into two groups. **This lesson teaches those letters formed with loops which are followed by a slant line.** The next lesson will teach the letters formed with loops followed by undercurves.

Teach the children first how to form the loop well. The loop is a somewhat difficult form, yet all it takes is practice. They should learn to make the loop sufficiently large, not simply a very small, round circle on the end of a curve. Explain to the children that, really, a loop is just two curves put together in a special way. You make a short undercurve that goes down to the middle line, then an overcurve that touches the end of the undercurve and goes on up to the top line. **Have the children practice this form on the blackboard until they can make it well.**

Go over the strokes and formation of the cursive-loop letters from this lesson on the blackboard with the children.

The letter *U* is made with a loop, slant, undercurve, slant, and undercurve. Show the children how the loop and the slant join together. The basic strokes of this letter are simple, and the children should have very little problem with it.

The letter *Y* is made with a loop, slant, undercurve, slant, and overcurve. The first part of the letter is formed exactly like the letter *U*. The second slant goes below the line, and a long loop is formed by the final overcurve.

The letter *V* is made with a loop, slant, and double curve. Be sure the children make the slant straight. The slant should stop just before it gets to the bottom line, and the first part of the double curve should touch the bottom line. The two sides of the letter should be fairly close together.

The letter *N* is made with a loop, slant, overcurve, slant, and undercurve. One thing you will need to help the children do is get the hump the right height. It is not to go all the way up to the top line, but should drop down from the top line a short distance.

The letter *M* is made with a loop, slant, overcurve, slant, overcurve, slant, and undercurve. This letter is formed like *N*, except it has an extra hump. The second hump drops even farther from the top line than the first. The children should be careful to make the two humps the same width, and in general as symmetrical as possible except for the height.

The letter *H* is made with a loop, slant, overcurve, slant, overcurve, and undercurve. This letter takes a little care in making, especially the last part. The two overcurves differ somewhat from the standard form, the first going from top to bottom and the second slanting backward rather than forward. The children need to be careful to bring the first overcurve down the proper distance away from the first slant line before beginning the second slant. They must also be sure the small loop in the middle of the letter just touches the first slant line, no more and no less.

The letter *K* is made with a loop, slant, double curve, overcurve, slant, and undercurve. With this letter the children will need to be careful to start the double curve at the right place so that it curves neatly to the exact middle of the first slant line. They should also be sure to make the second slant line straight.

Have the children practice these letters on the blackboard as you call out their strokes. Help them where you see they are uncertain or incorrect in formation.

*The children should copy each letter in the space following. Except for *K,* they should copy each stroke layout in the space immediately below. The stroke layout of *K* should be copied in the space following it.

Lesson 56
Learning Cursive Capitals With Loops (Part 2)

Lesson 56 Learning Cursive Capitals with Loops (Part 2)

117

Aim of the Lesson

To teach the children to form neatly the cursive-loop capitals that begin with a loop and a curve.

Instructions for the Teacher

This lesson teaches the loop capitals in which the loop is followed by a curve. Demonstrate this combination on the blackboard in its two forms—first as in the first four letters, then as in the last two.

The loop-undercurve combination as it is made in the letters *Q, Z, X,* and *W* should join smoothly and have an even curve. Have the children practice this combination by itself a number of times, before you look at each letter individually.

The letter *Q* is made with a loop, undercurve, and double curve. There is a fairly large loop where the undercurve and double curve join. The bottom part of the letter is much like the letter *L*. You may want to call the children's attention to this fact.

The letter *Z* is made with a loop, undercurve, undercurve, and overcurve. It also makes a small loop in the middle, which is smaller than the loop of the letter *Q*. The children will need to learn to make this letter straight backed, so that one could draw a regular slant line down the right side of the letter which would touch both undercurves at their farthest point. Some children have a tendency to make this letter curved in, especially at the bottom. Be sure the bottom loop is made accurately, with the two curves crossing exactly at the bottom line.

The letter *X* is made with a loop, undercurve, overcurve, and undercurve. The basic forms of this letter are not difficult to make, but it may be difficult to get them joined well in the middle. Here carefulness and accuracy are quite important. The overcurve-undercurve combination should appear as one large smooth curve without a point at the bottom.

The letter *W* is made with a loop, undercurve, undercurve, slant, and overcurve. This letter is fairly simple to make because it contains a slant line. With this letter watch that the second undercurve does not separate too far from the first undercurve. If it does, it will make the letter too wide and spread out. Also be careful that proper slant is being preserved in the letter.

The letter *T* is made with a loop, double curve, double curve, and undercurve. The letters *T* and *F* are very difficult to form accurately, and your children will not do a perfect job at first. First have them practice the top (loop-double curve combination) until they are fair at it before you have them attach the bottom part, which is not so difficult. Show them how the second double curve swings up sharply after touching the bottom line. Be sure they do not allow the top and bottom parts of the letter to touch.

The letter *F* is made with a loop, double curve, double curve,

undercurve, and short slant. The letters *T* and *F* are identical except that with *F* the undercurve crosses the second double curve and is followed by a short slant.

The children should practice each of these letters, preferably on the blackboard, before doing the lesson in the book.

*The letters should be copied in the space following each one and each stroke layout copied on the line immediately below.

Practice Sentences

1. Jesus blessed the children.
2. The rich young man went away sad.
3. Jesus came to serve others.

Lesson 57
Cursive Capitals With Ovals and *D*

Lesson 57 Cursive Capitals With Ovals and *D*

119

Aim of the Lesson

To teach the children to form the letters made with large ovals accurately and neatly.

Instructions for the Teacher

Begin the class period with warmup exercises in the air or on the blackboard. First have the children make several large retrace ovals and several large multiple slant lines ("ups and downs"). Next have them make several small letter *l*'s.

Introduce the two letters that are made with ovals by reminding the children of some things about the oval. The oval is not a circle. It is "squashed" sideways, and it is slanted. The overcurve and undercurve are made from the oval.

The letter *O* is formed with a large oval and an undercurve. Be sure the children close the oval at the top without a gap. The undercurve is not to come up to the top line, but it is to touch the middle line. This letter is very simple, but has much value as a practice letter in helping the children get the feel of the oval.

The letter *A* is formed with a large oval, a slant, and an undercurve. Explain to the children that capital *A* is like small *a* in most ways, except that capital *A* has no beginning overcurve stroke. Naturally, the oval is twice as big, and the slant line is twice as high. You will want to emphasize that this letter should be closed at the top, since many students become careless with this.

The letter *D* is made with a double curve, double curve, overcurve, and undercurve. This letter is an irregular one that really does not fit into any of the letter groups. It is the only letter that begins with a double curve, and it starts just below the top line. At the end of the first double curve is a small loop where the second double curve begins. The line continues out, up, and around to the top. A small final undercurve curves down to touch the beginning point before swinging down to the middle line and up to finish the letter.

After you have demonstrated and explained **each letter, have the children practice them either on practice paper or on the blackboard.** Supervise their work carefully.

*In this lesson the children should copy the stroke layouts of the first three letters on the lines immediately below. Each letter, including *T* and *F*, should be copied in the space that follows. *T* and *F* are included in this lesson to give the children more practice with these more difficult letters.

Lesson 58
Cursive Capitals Beginning With Reverse Loops and With Overcurves

Lesson 58 Cursive Capitals With Reverse Loops and With Overcurves

121

Aim of the Lesson

To teach the children to make neatly and accurately the two capital letters which begin with reverse loops and the two capital letters that begin with overcurves.

Instructions for the Teacher

These four capital letters are divided into **two groups. The first two letters, *C* and *E*, begin with a regular loop which is made facing backward. The letters *I* and *J* begin with simple overcurves.** They are the only capitals that do so.

Discuss and demonstrate each letter separately and **have the children practice each one in the air at some point in the discussion** of each letter.

The letter *C* is made with a loop, overcurve, and undercurve. Often students will try to make this letter as one big round stroke. Doing this makes it difficult to get a neat and correct form for the letter. Help the children to make the letter stroke by stroke rather than as a whole letter. First the reverse loop should be made to the top line, next the overcurve to the bottom line, then the final undercurve to the middle line.

The letter *E* is made with a loop, overcurve, (small) undercurve, overcurve, and undercurve. This letter again should be made stroke by stroke rather than as a few hastily drawn curves. Also be sure the children give this letter sufficient slant. One should be able to draw a regular slant line that touches the farthest points of the curves on the left side of the letter. Help your children make both curves of the letter smoothly.

The letter *I* is made with an overcurve, undercurve, and undercurve. This letter may be somewhat more difficult for the children to make and should therefore receive much practice. It also needs to have a good slant. Call the children's attention to the first undercurve in particular. Explain that this curve becomes sharper toward the bottom of the letter and gives it a boatlike appearance.

The letter *J* is made with an overcurve, slant, and overcurve. One important thing to watch is that the slant line is kept straight. Your children will have a tendency to curve it, but you must correct that tendency. The top loop should also be slightly larger than the bottom loop. Make sure the children's loops do not differ greatly from proper loop size. Also be sure both overcurves cross the slant line exactly at the bottom line.

Each letter should be practiced by the children on the blackboard or on practice paper before the lesson in the workbook is begun.

*In the lesson the children should copy the stroke layout of each letter in the space immediately below and fill the space following with copies of the letter. They should practice the “ups and downs” drill in row nine to the end of the row.

Practice Sentences

1. People asked Jesus questions.
2. Which is the first commandment of all?
3. Thou shalt love the Lord thy God.

Lesson 59
Review

Lesson 59 Review

Jesus died for our sins.

He was buried in a tomb.

Then He rose from death.

Soon He will come again.

O

123

Aim of the Lesson

To review slant and cursive strokes and letters.

Instructions for the Teacher

In this lesson the children will review the slant print small and capital letters, and the cursive small letters. The children have learned the basic forms of the cursive capital letters, but because they have not had much time to learn them thoroughly, you do not need to spend much time reviewing them. **Concentrate rather on the cursive small letters.** (The vertical manuscript letters will not be reviewed either, since we will expect the children to use slant print instead.)

Have the children look at the sentence in slant print. Send them to the blackboard to write several words in slant print. If they make mistakes in formation, correct them, and have them continue writing until they have attained a fair degree of accuracy. Be sure they remember to make ovals, not circles; and **watch their alignment.**

Next have them review the cursive strokes. They should practice the ovals and "ups and downs," then the individual strokes: the oval, undercurve, overcurve, double curve, slant, retrace, and loop.

Move on to the cursive letters themselves. Review the strokes of cursive letters by having the children give you the stroke formation of various letters orally. You could also give stroke descriptions of various letters as you make them in the air, then have them tell you what letter you are describing. (Note: Small *e* and *l* have the same stroke formation.)

The children should practice some of the more difficult cursive letters (such as *b, k, r,* and *z*) on the blackboard without looking at the book. Give them letters that you know they need practice on.

Give a final posture reminder. Explain how proper posture, pencil holding, and paper placement have much to do with neat writing and may help them to get a good grade in penmanship as well as in other subjects.

*In the lesson have the children copy each sentence once in the space directly below. On the last line they should copy and retrace ovals in the first space and make "ups and downs" to fill the last space.

Lesson 60
Test

Lesson 60 Test

1. 2.

3. 4. 5. 6. 7. 8. 9.

10. 11. 12.

13. 14. 15.

16. a. b. c. d. e. f.

17. 18.

19. 20.

125

Instructions for the Teacher

For this test, have the children clear their desks. Be sure they have good posture, are holding their pencils correctly, and have their test papers slanted correctly. Explain that they are to do their very best work on this test. Do not allow them to erase. Give them time to write the answer to each problem, spelling words orally as necessary.

Test

1. Write the word *Adam* in slant print.
2. Write the sentence "God is here" in slant print.

3. Write the numerals *4, 5,* and *8.*

4–9. Write these cursive strokes: (4) large oval, (5) small undercurve, (6) slant, (7) double curve, (8) small overcurve, (9) loop.

10. Write two cursive small letters that begin with overcurves.
11. Write two cursive small letters with upper loops.
12. Write two cursive small letters with lower loops.
13. Write one cursive small letter whose top comes just above the middle line.
14. Write two cursive small letters with ovals.
15. Write one cursive capital letter that begins with a loop.
16. Which of these should you be careful to do in writing? (Have them put down *T* for *true* and *F* for *false.*)
    a. Make sure your letters have the right slant.
    b. Always write with a yellow pencil.
    c. Make your letters even across the tops and firmly resting on the bottom line.
    d. Make your letters neatly only when someone is watching you.
    e. Make all the letters in a word the same distance apart.
    f. Put crosses on small *t*'s and dots above small *i*'s and *j*'s.
17. Write the word *cake* in cursive writing.
18. Write the word *zoo* in cursive writing.
19. Write this letter in slant print: *k*. (Write the cursive form on the blackboard, and have them translate it into slant print on their papers.)
20. Write this sentence in cursive: "I want to write to please God."

Grading the Test

In numbers 1–3, check for correct formation, spacing between words and letters, and alignment.

In numbers 4–9, be sure they have the correct strokes and have made them accurately.

In numbers 10–15, be sure they have the right letters and have made them accurately.

In number 16, the correct answers are *T, F, T, F, T, T.*

In numbers 17–20, check for accurate letter formation, proper slant, proper alignment, and punctuation. In number 19, be sure they have the right letter.

Do not take off for incorrect spelling, slight wavers in lines, or alignment that is off a millimeter. In other words, do not be too picky. *Do* take off for obvious and definite error or too much lack of precision. Count an entire answer wrong if there are two or more obvious errors per word; count it one-half wrong if there is one error per word. If the answer is a single letter, count the problem wrong if there is one error or more. Grade as you would any other assignment, counting twenty-five answers.

Slant Print Stroke Formations